primary music

LATER YEARS

joanna glover • susan young

UK   The Falmer Press, 1 Gunpowder Square, London, EC4A 3DE
USA   The Falmer Press, Taylor & Francis Inc., 325 Chestnut Street, 8th Floor, Philadelphia,
PA 19106

First published in 1999

A catalogue record for this book is available from the British Library

Library of Congress Cataloging-in-Publication Data are available on request

ISBN 0 7507 0646 5 paper

Design by Carla Turchini
Printed by TJ International Ltd, Padstow Cornwall

acknowledgments:

The following copyright holders have granted permission to reproduce music and
words:
The British Library for *Canon in Honour of Henry VIII* (Royal MC 11 E>XI, ff2V,
3), *Sumer is icumen in* (HARLEY MS 978, f11V) and Robert Parson's *In Nomine*
(ADD MS 31390 ff24V, 25). Reproduced by permission of The British Library.

Dragonfly Music for Farandole from Encyclopaedia Blowzabellica, The Blowzabella
Tune and Dance Book. Copyright 1987 Blowzabella/Dragonfly Music. Used by
permission of Dragonfly Music.

Novello and Co. Ltd. for 'Riddle me Ree' from *Rory's Rounds* by Nicola Lefanu.
Copyright 1984.

Schott and Co. Ltd. for the translation of the text of 'Kol dodi' from *Simply Sung* by
Mary Goetze. Copyright 1984 to Schott and Co. Ltd.

Every effort has been made to trace the ownership of all copyrighted material and to
secure the necessary permissions, but if any have been overlooked the publishers will
be pleased to make the necessary arrangements.

contents

to
Alexander
and Michael

acknowledgments

with thanks to
Nicola Bailey
Myra Barretto
Sue Edge
Jane Grey
Mairi Lanyon
Sandra Leyfield
Joy King
Brenda Kirwan
Jo McNally
Sharon Tozer
Kay Vernon
Graham Welch

and all the teachers and children.

photographs: Colin Evans
music copyist: Janet Lunt
photography at these schools:
Downsview Primary School, Croydon (Headteacher: John Corder)
St. Giles School, Croydon (Headteacher: Jackie Thomas)
Elmwood Junior School, Croydon (Headteacher: Heather Jones)

primary music: later years

music 7–11

The 7–11 age-phase is a time of great opportunity in children's musical development and also a time of enormous change. These four years see children move from the intuitive musical world of early childhood, through a middle childhood period which is often relatively calm, and on into the beginnings of adolescent engagement with the music of youth culture and adult society. This is such a major transition that it is hard for music provision in the primary school to move fast and freely enough to keep up with it.

The seven year old arrives at the middle years of schooling bringing a rich and varied background of musical experiences, including three or four years of early years music education and the musical experiences of home and community accumulated since birth. This resource of musical skills, understanding and knowledge, individual to each child, together with personal interests and enthusiasms for music must all be reckoned with at the point of transfer. Only by taking careful account of what has gone before can the teacher take the first steps in preparing for children's music learning during this later primary age phase.

From birth, babies and young children are acute listeners, taking in all the musical sounds they hear around them in the home, nursery and the community. Over the years, the seven year old has listened to and absorbed an enormous wealth and variety of musical sound. This store of remembered musical experiences feeds the musical imagination and supports musical skill learning. As well as being immersed in a musical environment, small children are sung to and invited to take part in musical games with caring adults, in the family and beyond. There are lullabies, toddler games, early years singing games, tapes and CDs, and TV programmes with interactive music activities for children to join in. From the youngest age the child responds to interactive music play with voice sounds and body movements. In their own play, children sing spontaneously, move and dance, and bang and tap rhythmically with toys, enjoying the sounds. The young child's musical activity is playful and intuitive, a direct response to sound and to movement which, if fostered in early music educational experiences, can form the foundations of their music learning. This quality is vital to all musical experience, of whatever kind and at all ages, and being playful with music is not lost in the later years of primary school, but widened to include reflection and analysing.

Young children set their own directions and are not easily diverted. The early years teacher has developed skills of observing and listening in order to discover the young child's self-directed music activity, to connect with and extend it. At the same time, new experiences and skill extensions are carefully introduced: songs to sing, movements and ideas for dancing, music to listen to, instruments to listen to, play, learn about and so on. And the child's skills are built in keeping with what is known of children's developmental pathways in each of these areas. Thus the child's contribution and the input introduced by the teacher are kept in careful balance. This basis of observation and listening, which guides teaching decisions by giving the teacher insight into each child's learning, runs strongly throughout all the primary years. Lacing the child's own musical activity in composing and performing with the development of a whole range of musical skills is a two-sided process which requires careful management. At the same time, through investigations, the child's work is vitalised by contact with many musics. Allowing children to tread their own individual musical pathway through the later years of primary school is a delicate and difficult challenge for all teachers.

During the 7–11 phase, many children's growing competence and capacity for acquiring new skills is energised by an enthusiasm, curiosity and will to learn that is readily turned to music given even the smallest encouragement. Children who are struggling for numerous reasons – academically, socially, or with behaviour, learning, or home difficulties – often find support and enjoyment in music that can significantly contribute to their wider development. Music is already a vital force in most children's lives beyond school. The challenge is for music in school to connect audibly with the music world beyond and to have enough richness and strength to continue drawing on the child's already engaged interest and motivation throughout this time.

During this age phase, children may develop quite clearly defined personal interests and be ready to pursue these in a systematic way. This may take the form of joining a music group, learning to play a particular, chosen instrument, or having dance lessons. This is a prime time for acquiring basic skills and learning fast on a tide of enthusiasm and teachers have a key role in encouraging and supporting these initiatives. It is also intrinsic to the nature of musical activity that musical skills are differentiated and diverse. Every instrument is different, every style has its own demands, the range of skills involved in composing, performing and listening is vast. It is desirable, and, more than that, inevitable that children will pursue music learning in different ways. This is a challenge that primary schools have to face if real progress is to be achieved as the children move on. It is also a challenge to maintain equal opportunities and open access to music for all children. The polarisation of children into 'the musicians' and 'the rest' is deeply damaging to all and it is during this phase that it can emerge, often, sadly, fostered by schools themselves. It is important that each and every child sees themselves as musically capable and that the music curriculum has enough breadth to be inclusive, both in the classroom and across the extended curriculum of clubs and groups.

For the later primary years class teacher, then, the focus is on uncovering and building on groundwork already laid, working on a basis of the experiences children bring so that each child's individual musical development is sustained right through to the next point of transfer, that is, into secondary school. This book aims to pick up the developmental learning strands of the young child at the end of the early years phase (Young and Glover, 1998) and look closely at provision for music learning through the later primary years. A key concern is with the progression of each child as an individual within the class group and with a broad and well balanced provision for every child across this extraordinary age-span.

The book offers a series of discussions and practical suggestions concerning key issues in music learning and provision for the 7–11 age-group. Each section explores the issues surrounding a specific aspect of music learning, and, where relevant, gives outlines of practical work as examples of how the approaches suggested here might be adopted by class teachers. These are accompanied by 'planning points' which show how provision in practical terms of time, space and opportunity can be managed. Indications of how work relates to children's individual progression in developing musical skills, knowledge and understanding are given at the end of each practical section. Assessment points follow and are also brought together at the end of the book.

If music in school is to connect with the wider world of contemporary music in which children and teachers find themselves, it is vital first to consider some aspects of how music beyond school relates to primary music education.

school music and beyond

One of the most exciting, if most challenging, aspects of working in music with children is the sheer diversity of the musical worlds in which we all now live. In approaching planning for music in the later primary years, some thought needs to be given to the implications of this diversity in relation to the whole school approach to music.

If a school can establish a musical ethos which is alive in its response to the range of music children encounter beyond school in the wider community, the quality of children's musical experience and learning is very much enhanced. This becomes a key issue for the 7–11 age-group as they move towards an awareness of musical style, culture and difference and become increasingly concerned with how their own musical activity relates to the music they hear around them. Central to this concern, of course, is how the music sounds. For the teacher, with a still wider perspective on musical diversity in terms of style, time and place, there is an important role in making sure that musical experiences in school do connect with, and make reference to, the musical worlds beyond. School music needs to recognise the range of popular, jazz, folk/ traditional and classical/art musics which are heard live and across the media, as well as acknowledging the range of contexts in which music is found – for entertainment, in religious practice, among different social groups, and linked to dance, work or recreation.

It is from the everyday experiences of music in most peoples' lives that a shared sense of music's value comes. It may be hard for anyone to articulate exactly what this value is, and accounts will differ widely from one person to another, but to some extent there is a widespread recognition that music matters to most of us, and in many diverse ways. A school, and above all the staff of a school, can represent this for children through the ways in which music is chosen, heard, responded to, spoken of and valued. If teachers allow their musical selves to show, they inevitably model a diversity and a musical reality which helps children to grow in their own musical personas. Personal musical interests become related to the school music situations in which teachers work. Each staff member brings their own musical life which is integrated into the ethos of the school as a place for music. The musical messages are positive; children can see that music is part of life, that behaving musically is part of adult identity, and that there are many equally valuable ways to be musically active. If, on the other hand, music in the school is represented solely by a rather slight strand of units and weekly lessons and a repertoire attached to and owned by nobody, it is hard for children to widen their understanding of the deeper aspects of music and its meaning for people in the wider cultural context.

Valuing, modelling and including diversity in music in school is most important of all in relation to the provision of a curriculum based on equal opportunities, one in which all children can feel comfortable in relating their music learning in school to their experience of music in the home and outside school generally. Gender, race, religion and social and cultural backgrounds can all carry strong musical values and practices; some continuity is necessary between the overall picture of music presented by a school and children's own musical biographies beyond. It will be hard for a child to make good progress in learning if music as he or she knows it simply doesn't find a place on the school's musical map. Models are powerful in opening up opportunities for children, particularly in cutting across gender or racial bias. A school operating with an inclusive approach to the music curriculum also enables everyone to widen their outlook and learn from difference. It enables individuals each to recognise some way in which they can participate and can help children to cross musical boundaries with awareness and confidence. In this way, opportunities can be extended.

It may seem that this faces any one primary school with an impossible role. It is certainly an ongoing task to sustain openness of attitudes and gradually build resources and a broadly-based understanding. It is not, however, a matter of trying to represent or teach aspects of all kinds of music all the time. Rather it is the ethos of the school as a whole which can develop on a basis of looking outwards, making space for range and difference and then drawing on the particular strengths represented by the school community itself – teachers, pupils, parents and friends. The pooled resource of music skills, interests and knowledge possessed by staff members as a group is likely to provide a reserve of music skills, enthusiasms and creativity which is seldom drawn on as fully as it might be. In a single school, staff musical strengths and interests may include opera, travel and world musics, guitar playing and folk groups, several orchestral instruments, choral singing, musicals, and dance ranging from tap to Arabic dance and salsa.

Schools are often under-using this kind of whole-staff potential, preferring to rely on the skills of one specialist teacher than draw on those of all staff. Yet however well trained and broad in interests, one teacher presents only one musical personality. Making the most of what each staff member is able to contribute allows for a wider range of working styles in music. It is not acceptable for schools to offer only a single, narrowly defined musical direction for all pupils.

If it is a belief within the school that music is for all children, then it must be born out among the adults in the school also. Primary school staff are multi-skilled practitioners, used to pooling their capabilities. The traditional model of the specialist teacher who does all the music carries the danger of obscuring the varied and interesting musical potential in the school as a whole. The alternative model, of music team work and joint responsibility for music focuses upon the musicality and creativity of each member and how it can be released. An egalitarian climate for music teaching is built on shared vision and principles and recognises different abilities and interests shaping individual styles of teaching. The subject leader's role is to develop this 'differentiated teaching' rather than to monopolise. Each class teacher can then feel confident that they have their own musical skills and understanding to contribute in teaching music with their own class in addition to any specialist input that may be made.

All this has a bearing on how music in the school sounds. Ideally, school music will sound varied and a range of musical styles will be clear and recognisable. There is no such thing as a 'standard' music in the way we think of 'standard' English. And there is no music which stands completely outside any particular musical style, being as it were stylistically neutral. Music can cross styles, adapt or combine them; indeed musical fusions are a rich ground for experimentation and creativity, whether in popular, world or classical music spheres. But working with music or listening to it always involves understanding style, whether consciously or not.

And because culturally we are now used to such a wide range of musical styles, this becomes an important factor in music education, particularly during the later primary age-phase when children's aural awareness of musical style develops very fast.

Much emphasis is placed in music teaching on introducing children to the elements of music – timbre, texture, pitch, duration and so on – and to the musical structures – melody, rhythm, harmony, form which build from those elements. How music is made and how elements and structures are used is always relative to musical style. None of the elements or structures of music can be learned or taught without engaging with them from within one or more musical styles. In fact it would be more accurate to say that musical style is defined by the way certain elements or structures are used. What tells the listener that the music heard is by McCartney, Maconchy or Mozart is the combination of particular and characteristic melodic, rhythmic etc. ways in which the composer structures the music. 'Characteristic' here may refer to music of a particular time, a place, a musical genre as well as to the personal style of the composer, or even of the composer at a particular stage in her or his career.

Style is a much wider concept than simply a structural one, however. Musical styles encompass whole sets of behaviour, both musical and otherwise, and are intricately linked to the wider cultural context within which music takes place and develops. We are all familiar with the ways in which musical style links to lifestyle, both in a commercial sense, e.g. in relation to contemporary fashion or dance, say, and in a much deeper community sense e.g. in relation to groups of people belonging to certain religions, or living outside their country of origin, or under oppressive regimes. Musical performance itself is intrinsically style-related. This is the case at every level from the production of the sound and the use of timbre, to, for example, techniques of singing or playing, ways of interpreting melody and rhythm, the precise pitching of scales and sets of notes, the forms of decoration or improvisation which the performer contributes, and the kinds of interactions between musicians. The influence of style extends to the ways in which performances are presented – where, when, how, for whom – and to the audience behaviour considered appropriate, e.g. sitting silently, dancing, head-banging, calling out, joining in.

It is all too easy for the music children experience in school to take on a sound (a style) all of its own, bearing little resemblance to any actual style of any actual music they hear anywhere else. This can happen, for instance, if the school singing has a uniform kind of speed and tone, perhaps a drone- or chant-like kind of delivery which is heard on all singing occasions, whatever the song. It may be that instruments used are entirely poor quality 'school' instruments, even toy instruments such as band trolleys often carry. Or there may be little proper listening to live or recorded performances of a range of different music, and little careful listening *within* music making activities. Under these conditions school music can become a house style all of its own.

In approaching the planning of music for the 7–11 age-range, some thought needs to be given, therefore, to the implications of all this for both the sound and images of music throughout the school, to how music is represented and by whom. An awareness of musical style and diversity is essential to promoting lively, strong, varied and appropriate musical behaviour and responses. It is also a way of ensuring that 'school music' has continuity with the 'real' world of music beyond.

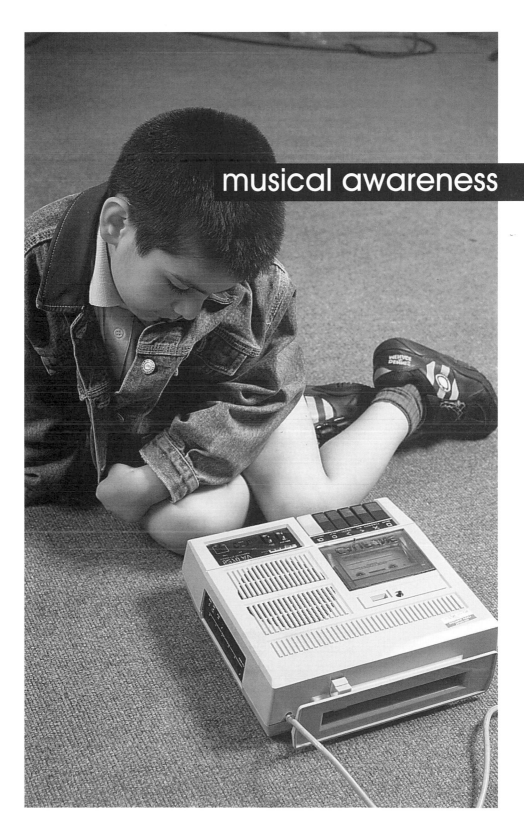

musical awareness

primary music: later years

Very often it is the practical aspects of music which, understandably, attract most attention in planning the curriculum. The focus is on ideas for sequences of activities, resources and materials, since in the end it is through these that the curriculum is taught. Clearly, planning what to do is important and has to be realistic and practical. Decisions about practice must, however, be dependent on a clear understanding of the kind and quality of music learning which is being planned for in the long term. What is at issue here is not only which singing, playing, composing, listening, dancing, or appraising activities are to be carried out but, much more crucially, how they are to be approached and with what learning objectives in sight. At the core of all music learning is the development of what can broadly be termed 'musical awareness'.

This section draws attention to some fundamental issues in developing musical awareness. Two aspects of musicality which need to remain central if music learning is to be of high quality in fostering this awareness are:

● the development of musical imagination and creativity; and
● the development of perceptive and responsive listening.

A third dimension, that of learning how to use language in a musical context, underpins much musical understanding and the ability to interact musically with others.

The extent to which children are enabled to develop these facets of their inner musical sense and intelligence will determine the quality of their work and the scope of their understanding. Keeping this in mind is intrinsic to ensuring that practical activities have musical depth and purpose. In planning for music in school, then, it is crucial to consider how listening, imagination, creativity and language are being fostered and to aim to ensure that the way in which any and all music work is undertaken allows these to remain core concerns. In assessing each child's music learning, these aspects are key indicators of the quality and value of work achieved.

creativity and imagination

Music with children should feel creative. It should feel creative for both children and teachers, since if musical creativity is lost then the music is lost too. Yet the sense of music as a creative art can become very tenuous in the classroom situation. It is all too easy for it to become submerged in the rush to move on as fast as possible, or in a style of teaching in which any creative aspects of the work, the choice of instruments to accompany singing, for example, are controlled entirely by the teacher. Key questions for the quality of music in a school are those of how to encourage children in working creatively and how to sustain an immediate and vivid sense of music as an art.

From the youngest age, teachers can expect and encourage children to work in music in ways which are inventive, imaginative, innovative and responsive. They can foster children's ability to generate their own purposes and ideas and to become tenacious and increasingly skilful in following these through the stages of experimentation, development and realisation in a communicable form. Across the whole range of children's composing, listening and performing activity, teachers can expect and look for divergent ideas and responses. They can help children to develop a heightened musical awareness and sensitivity – to raw sound, to sound images and to musical shapes, structures, ideas and forms. It is in this aural awareness that creativity is rooted. Above all, teachers can make sure that all children remain confident as individuals in using their own musical imaginations and in sharing their creative ideas with others.

During the 7–11 age phase, a very significant development is in the extent to which children can begin to see their own musical creativity as such, to understand that they can take decisions which affect the musical outcome as other people perceive it. This growing awareness of their own and others' creative imagination opens the way for making comparisons and for the development of their own aesthetic judgments about musical outcomes. The consequences of this can appear to be somewhat erratic as tastes swing between a desire for conformity to particular sound ideals, which themselves can be various, ill-assorted and ever-changing, and the growing courage to pursue new-found 'visions' independently. This stage requires considerable support from teachers who can consistently sustain

13

children in keeping faith with their own judgment whilst making available plenty of help, models, and judgments of their own when asked for.

'Nothing ever comes from nothing'. For children's musical imaginations to develop they need rich and varied musical experiences from which to draw. Taking in perceptions of musical sound images, learning to hear these 'in your head', being able to conjure up musical ideas in mind which can be realised in actual sound later – these are all functions of the imagination which play a key part in musical creativity. Annie (8) described the way she composes in these terms:

> *'I have ideas and put them into my head, then put them altogether'*.

This comment is interesting because it shows a sense of internalising sound images in the way that is so crucial to imaginative composing.

Disconcertingly, Sartre (1940) described the image, the object of imaginative consciousness, as suffering from 'a sort of essential poverty'. Whereas in perception 'there is always, at each and every moment, infinitely *more* than we see' and 'to exhaust the wealth of my actual perception would require infinite time', by contrast in imagination 'the object of the image is never more than the consciousness one has of it …nothing can be learned from an image that is not already known'. This view belongs to a very particular philosophical approach resting on a whole theory of consciousness. It is perhaps interesting and salutary, however, to be confronted by such a reversal of the more familiar characterisations of perception and imagination: of perception as limited and imagination as boundless. Arguably, it is the richness of perceptual experience on which richness of imagination rests.

In addition to drawing on the skills of thinking imaginatively with sound itself, working creatively in music demands much wider abilities to approach music-making and listening in inventive and exploratory ways and, as an intrinsic part of applying skills and knowledge, to make new and imaginative 'meanings' and interpretations. It was Einstein's observation that: 'imagination is more important than knowledge'.

The teaching skills needed to foster such abilities are identical to those needed in other areas of the curriculum where creativity is being looked for, whether in writing, science, art, history or design and technology. An attitude of valuing creativity, both across the curriculum and in music, is essential in working towards excellence.

All this implies approaches to listening, talking, singing, playing, composing and improvising which allow room for children's as well as teachers' creativity to be active. This might entail:

- having high expectations of every child as being able to contribute ideas from their own experience and imaginative resources;
- making time and opportunity for children to contribute their ideas in performing and discussion contexts, as well as in composing;
- giving children plenty of experience of seeing and hearing how other people work creatively in music, and a range of models to consider, including teacher-led modelling of creative processes;
- making opportunities for individuals to work through these same processes on the basis of their own skills and judgment and to reflect on processes as well as outcome.

Planning will need to include both time for working alone and class times which combine teacher-led activity with, for example, the teacher working in some depth in front of the class with the ideas of one child at a time. This is an alternative to the 'free for all' where lots of ideas are offered and either conglomerated into no-one's work or left as untried speculations. Despite the fact that children have turns in the spotlight much less often, over weeks rather than minutes perhaps, this approach has the advantage that all the children benefit from seeing how someone else's ideas are taken on, applied, developed and seen and heard through. This not only helps to share new perspectives; it also models the creative processes of trying out, listening and deciding. Interest is held when children can get inside issues or explorations; it is lost when everything is speedy and superficial. The teacher's role, therefore, moves between the functions of modelling, instructing and then handing over control, facilitating a child's work which is being driven by the child's own ideas. Enabling children to work creatively in music entails being open to the unforeseen and unforeseeable. There will be times when it is profitable to *teach on the verge of peril* (Murray Schafer, 1975, No. 3 of Maxims for Educators).

As a time-based art, music always has to be made, every time. The making process should whenever possible draw on children's ideas, fuelled by a gradually growing clarity of each individual's ways of doing it. Musical creativity is closely linked to our inner sense of musicality. Children will need encouragement to recognise and use this, to tap into their own inner musical energy as a source of ideas, and as a flow of energy shaping how they sing, play, how they make the music in the moment when it happens, how they feel the impact of it, or how they communicate and pick up on the same flow from others. This creativity is needed to generate musical ideas: for children as composers and when improvising. It is also needed as listeners notice, store images, think about them, interpret and reinterpret and as performers take the given music – song, dance, melody, rhythm and respond to it by creating it newly.

The term 'creative music' has sometimes been used narrowly in music education to refer just to improvisation and composition activities. This highlights the creative musical opportunities these vital aspects of music offer. It is not useful, however, if such terminology somehow reinforces an idea that performing music or listening to it does not also draw on musical creativity. It is essential that creativity lies at the heart of all musical activity with children. For example:

- When children learn a song, ask for reactions, responses, ideas about the song itself which might suggest ways of singing it; link this to learning techniques which help put ideas into practice; try different interpretations, different dynamic shapes, tones, speeds. '*Like this?*' Ask children to listen. '*Like that?*' Listen again. Ask for judgments based on listening responses. Sometimes the teacher can model this process, making it explicit. Sometimes, choose one child to make today's decisions according to their own judgment. Or listen to a recording of the song and ask '*what did this performer/conductor decide to do? what were they aiming at? why like this? what character does it give the music?*' and so on.

- When children listen to music, encourage them to appraise in a way that draws on their own speculation and imagination across different musical aspects. Ask, for example, '*what musical purposes or ideas did this composer have for this*

> *music?' 'what is the dramatic effect of the music on you? how has the composer made this happen?' 'what do you think the performers had most in their minds? what did they decide to do?'* Using a range of media – words, image, dance – for responding on different occasions allows different children to relate to the music in different ways. Sometimes model these or use responses of other writers, artists, critics, dancers, to model a creative response.

Many people's early musical education has substantially by-passed or under-valued any sense they had of their own musical creativity and this can cause difficulties for teachers and for children who absorb similar messages from adults around them. Behind this lies the failure to recognise that just as people are endlessly creative with language – in humour, in self-expression, in ordinary usage as well as in language-based arts, so they can be with music, given the opportunity. Many adults would not consider themselves capable of being creative or 'artistic' in a musical way. When teachers feel like this it becomes hard for them to know quite what they are trying to foster or how to do it.

As with most things, guesswork only reaches so far. In the end, insights into musical creativity, one's own and other people's, come from lots of close musical contact, observation, questioning and making.

The long term aim with children is to convey the idea that each person has their own musical imagination and their own ways of thinking and responding musically. But this aim can only be met by building up slowly from lots of small opportunities and by consistently expecting and accepting ideas, choice, and difference, from each child. Central to all this is listening.

listening

It's easy to forget that music is fundamentally about a special way of listening – and that developing skills of special listening is the prime aim of music education. Simply taking part in singing and playing or listening to recorded music does not automatically guarantee that children's aural awareness is being developed, although the children are busy and appear to be musically active. How can we teach to ensure that children learn to listen deeply and responsively?

Careful, perceptive listening, while essential for music learning and teaching, can also be developed in an ongoing way within the classroom to the benefit of the classroom environment and the learning which takes place within it. Circle time may emphasise the need for quiet so that one child is heard and others pay listening attention. A science investigation may involve noting small changes in sound as part of an observation. A child's poem reading for assembly may be improved by careful attention to voice tone and articulation. The challenge for the teacher is to create suitable conditions and focus children's attention so that concentrated listening can occur. This kind of work can build aural concentration in readiness for musical listening.

Perceptive listening thrives in the right conditions. Overload the ears in noisy environments and the aural sense partially shuts down in defence. It is unrealistic to expect children to listen with focused attention to sounds unless they are placed against a white background of silence. Such conditions may be difficult to achieve but in the long term less musical activity of better quality may be more valuable than compromises.

When music listening is really happening it needs time. As a result the musical activity which is seen and heard may slow down considerably giving an immediate impression that less is taking place. In fact, the best listening times may be when the children are almost immobile and focused intently on some small sounding moment. We are used to music work being counted as valuable if it is busy and hands-on and it may be difficult to be reassured of the value of three listeners in a group hunched around one child who is exploring the sonorities of a drum. The temptation is to think that these children are 'not doing anything'. Yet it is precisely these kinds of arrangements which will pocket the musical activity in silence for real listening to be able to happen and emphasise the essential role of listening in any musical activity. The children may appear to be less active and moving much more slowly through a task but in reality will be gaining more – this is the paradox. Teachers can choose children to be 'the listeners': *'We have two children working on a song this morning, who will be ready to go over and be their listeners when they need you?'* (Similarly teachers might encourage 'watchers' for dance.) They can model this role in their own teaching: *'I've come to be your listener, are you ready to play through what you have worked on so far?'* Not only does this approach promote the role of listener as a key one (and make the distribution of tasks and resources easier in management terms), it also gives children experience of stepping outside an activity in order to listen to it objectively. Centred in your own sound as player or singer it is difficult to be able to attend both to producing the sound and to listening carefully to the results. Music voice work, particularly, is so resonant within the body that we are often surprised at how it sounds to others. Feedback from outside is essential in learning to gauge just how our voice is sounding beyond our own physical sensations. It is a particularly helpful strategy to pair children, taking turns, so that one sings a song for the other to listen to and give comment. Similarly in composing, one child may be working on a xylophone and another arrives to listen and describe what they hear.

Aural awareness cannot be taught by direct instruction. It can only be supported by managing the conditions which foster it and, at the same time, modelling and prompting in words: *'listen carefully; are you really listening? try hard to take your ear down into the music and track the drum; close your eyes and listen hard – there, do you hear it?'* Expectations should be high. All too often listening demands are minimal and as a result do not hold the interest of the children. At this age they should be well beyond simple questions such as *'is it loud or soft, fast or slow?'* Listening for finer and finer detail, as if taking a magnifying glass to tiny musical differences will stretch the children's aural abilities. The aim is depth and detail rather than breadth and superficiality.

A class of children were choosing metal sounds for composition. Each of the instruments was listened to first during a whole class input session from the teacher. The two very slight differences in the tuning of each separate bell from a pair of Indian bells were discovered which then explained the sharp sensation to the ear as they were struck together; the aural equivalent of biting into a lemon. Having listened to the detail of that sound, the children had a lasting sensation, image and awareness which they take with them into all future work. From one example of the Indian bells the children then went away to transfer this same careful listening to each of the other instruments: *'do all the jingles on the tambourine have exactly the same sound or is the random jangle of metal part of the tambourine effect? does each side of the triangle give a similar sound? how should it be played to ring clearly?'*

In this example, the attention to specific sound detail was then released back into a real musical situation. It is not enough to assume that children will listen perceptively to instruments if left to explore and discover for themselves. They need to be coached in how to listen. The children were working on composing for certain kinds of metal sounds. In the preliminary preparation they listened to the qualities of instruments with the hope that they would use them with sensitivity in their own music. Listening skills are lifeless without application to real music-making situations. Just listening carefully to sounds is not of itself a musical activity, only a preparation for musical contexts in which children are using their aural sensitivity to their own creative ends.

There are different dimensions to aural awareness:
● the direct impact of sound upon the ear and the body;
  Sound hits the body and has a direct physiological effect on us: the chest-deep resonances of a giant gong, the skull-dry hardness of a woodblock. Physical sensations are a vital source of sound awareness, essentially so if hearing is impaired, but one which for all children can so easily be overlooked. Just listening, eyes closed and really feeling sounds at this physiological level can re-educate a sensitivity for sound which we all have but which perhaps becomes dulled.

● aural understanding;
  Aural understanding, being able to recognise what is listened to,

to analyse and identify, can only be built from a rich foundation of children's personal experience accumulated over considerable time. This process cannot be hurried. A musical idea which is pulled out and generalised by being named must emerge for children out of their own experiences of music. Once named it can be talked about, worked with, connected, found in other contexts, compared and in these ways musical understanding is extended. But naming is not knowing; aural knowledge can only be demonstrated in children's active musical behaviour. It can be tempting to short cut, to start with names, with concepts, as if they have a musical existence of their own – dynamics, tempo, an ostinato etc. But like fish out of water, these have no existence removed from real musical situations.

● aural imagination and decision-making.
Inner hearing, being able to think sounds in the head is an aspect of developing listening skills which needs specific attention. Listening perception feeds into aural imagination, being able to imagine sounds not yet heard. Again, the teacher needs to prompt and encourage, pausing to make a silence for children to practise thinking through what has just been heard in activities: 'play it – think it – play it again;' 'sing it – think it – sing it again;' 'listen to it – think it – listen to it again'. The various games which can be played with songs in which children keep silent for a portion of the song and then enter again, draw on the skills of reproducing the sound in mind alone. Imagination of what music might sound like can be prompted by something to look at – a drawing, numbers, patterns, score, some dancing, a silent video of players, something to feel – textures, objects, movements. Or it might be prompted by words – poetic words which describe, information words which tell, technical words which instruct. These can become stimuli for children's own work in time, firing up the aural imagination. The part that listening then plays in the composing process is impossible to underestimate. Almost all composing decisions will be made on the basis of sound; learning to listen carefully, to remember sound and to hold sound images in mind are fundamental composing skills.

Long term, the aim is to give children plenty of experience at making aural decisions, by putting them in situations in which they are able to use their listening skills and imagination together. Involving children in all kinds of musical problem solving which stretch aural awareness and imagination is important: *'Does it sound good to sing this note a little louder than all the others?' 'Will this rhythm played a little quicker make it sound more exciting?' 'How can you make this part sound more sombre and mysterious to fit with that part of the dance?'* Through being involved in such close listening, with the precise details of interpretation and how music is made, the learning potential of each musical encounter is exploited, and although less ground may be covered, the learning gains for children are far greater.

activities

The following quick activities focus on developing particular kinds of listening awareness and may help to introduce and highlight skill areas for practice. They cannot, however, stand in for the experience of using listening skills in the whole musical context. Challenge children to aim for a very high level of listening and control. By the later part of the age phase, children are able to be analytical about the skills involved and develop activities to include higher levels of challenge.

- Match a hand clap, or any other simple sound, passed round the music circle. Aim for identical timbre (quality of sound), dynamic and attack. Listen, discuss and negotiate how to improve as a group.
- Two players with the same instruments share a sustained sound, or repeating pattern, taking turns but aiming to sound like one. All listen and suggest ways of maintaining continuity and a uniform sound.
- Three players work with different instruments to produce: a) a balance of three sounds b) three sounds which blend completely c) three sounds resistant to balance or blend.

matching timbre, dynamics, texture

- Using beat based recorded music, pick out the beat with finger or foot tap and concentrate on matching, keeping in time, accuracy of every beat; discuss how steady the beat actually is, whether it speeds up or slows down at all, whether any players or singers stretch the rhythm against the beat. Describe the tempo resulting from the speed of the beat e.g. *lively, lazy*. Try examples which make subtle variations in tempo. Discuss the effect.
- Make a repeating hand/body pattern or very simple dance step to fit music which speeds up or slows down gradually; keep the pattern

going and adapt speed to fit exactly the changes as they happen; work with a partner who watches and listens and notices discrepancies.

feel of beat, tempo, different kinds of tempo change

- A leader gives assorted rhythm patterns for the rest of the group to copy back in a call and response format. Have one pattern, heard at the beginning, which no-one must copy so that the response is silent. Catch out anyone who forgets the chosen pattern and responds. (A version of 'Simon Says'.) Use different metres, counting in 3s, 4s, and 5s.

- A leader gives a rhythm pattern made of single beats and single rests,
  e.g. I I O I I O or, much harder, I I O I O I I O. The leader repeats the pattern, played on claves, or a drum while the group find the rests and clap only in these spaces. The group end up playing the pattern which interlocks with the original,
  e.g. O O I O O I or O O I O I O O I. Best done with eyes shut.

- A leader plays a repeating pattern based on mixed groups of twos and threes
  e.g. I I I I I I I I I I I
  　　 >　　>　　>　　>
  Other players join in with the first (accented) note only of each group when they've found it. Best done with eyes shut.

rhythm patterns, rests, metre

- Listen to a 2-note melodic 'move'. Reflect the difference between 'up', 'down', and 'stays the same' by any kind of body action.

- Zig-zag refers here to any 3 pitch melody shape. Match heard examples to zig-zag pitch shapes already drawn on cards, or draw pitch shapes as you listen in 'join the dots' fashion. Explore the shapes arising from larger or smaller jumps between pitches and expect accuracy about the size of these as well as the direction of the zig-zag.

- Listen to a solo melodic line, best if fairly slow moving; as you listen trace the outline contour in the air with your finger following as the melody moves higher and lower. Aim for accuracy not only in direction but in judging by how much it moves and keeping pitches which return level in spacing.

pitch, melody shape

- Someone hums a song for the rest of the group to guess, or hums a snatch only of melody from a known song, just the beginning or mid-way section, and asks the group to identify the song. (Name that tune).
- Find the set of notes on which a song is based. Establish the tonality of the song by singing up and down this tone-set slowly, listening carefully, before singing the full melody. Ask individuals to try finding and singing the tone-set of songs they know. Then sing the full melody.
- Isolate wide melodic jumps or difficult turns of melody from known songs. Model the singing, focus the group's listening on the precise intervals and then ask them to echo. Discuss what makes it hard and continue practice, returning extracts to the context of the whole song sung again.
- Sing a known song; at a signal from the leader, sing silently in your head, then, at another signal, sing out aloud again. (Can be 'Traffic Lights', using red and green signals.)
- Pick out a known song melody on an instrument by ear, with or without a given set of notes or a starting note.

song melodies, song tonality, internalising singing

- Mark the end of each phrase in a piece of music sung or played by making a particular movement, individually or as a group e.g. close open hands, turn to face outside or inside of circle, change walking direction.
- Find a piece with simple and not too frequent chord changes or ask someone to improvise one, perhaps using the auto-chord facility on a keyboard. The group signal chord changes as they hear them or small groups move in turn only when they hear their own assigned chord.
- Make a simple dance (folk style, line or disco routine) to a given piece of music matching musical repetitions to repeating movements to show the structure of the piece.

structure linked to phrase, harmony and form

- Lie down and listen to sounds all around. A leader can focus this with questions to be answered silently e.g. *'what is the farthest away sound you can hear?'*. Or stop and close eyes to absorb the soundscape of a new place just visited e.g. city street, railway station, natural environment, entrance to a museum.
- Listening to a previously heard piece of music change stone into other hand each time you lose concentration.

~ Sometimes just listen to music, as to a story, with no instructions and no requirements, lying or sitting comfortably, or with eyes closed and head on hands at a table.

different kinds of listening attention

language

As a learning tool underlying the development of awareness and understanding, language is as important in music learning as in any curriculum area. It is useful therefore for a school staff to review how language is taught and used in the musical context and to plan for language development as part of all musical activity. In the early years of schooling, it is easy to keep children's language needs in focus because their lack of vocabulary and of basic conceptual understanding makes this an inescapably foreground issue. As children gather experience and develop a basic repertoire of musical vocabulary and concepts it can become harder for the teacher to maintain the impetus to enrich and extend these. Yet to a considerable extent the development of children's musical thinking continues to go hand in hand with the development of language use in a musical context.

vocabulary based on musical elements

For most pupils the 7–11 age phase includes a major part of the shift which Sloboda (1985) describes as 'the progress from enactive to reflective knowledge'. He suggests that the main developmental trend in music between the ages of five to ten is 'the increasing reflective awareness of the structures and patterns that characterise music and which are already implicit in the child's enactive repertoire' (ibid.). The seven year old is still in the process of developing basic musical concepts, particularly perhaps those which are related to pitch, that is, concepts of melody and harmony, and those which arise from music's time-based structures, those of form and temporal change. For some children, the process of acquiring this beginning understanding of each of the musical elements and some basic ways in which to draw on this in talking about music is still taking place as they reach the end of primary schooling. Other ten and eleven year olds are well advanced in their ability to talk analytically about their own and others' music and can distinguish between and use different kinds of talk and writing about music in appropriate contexts. Teachers' expectations can be justifiably high on this front.

The following outline of vocabulary related to musical elements is adapted from Young and Glover (1998). It forms a basis for consideration of the range and kind of specific vocabulary which can be developed further with children as they move through this age-phase. Where children have had very little experience of talking about music, they will need time to adopt both the vocabulary and ways of using it, particularly since it has its own metaphors and imagery which, although familiar within the culture, are not immediately self-evident to children. For those who already have a sound early years basis, enrichment and extension should be the focus and this will take place in the context of a wider engagement with talking and writing about music as indicated later in this section.

Timbre: *the sound of sound, the quality of the sound itself.*
Use any adjectives which can conjure up sound. Of all the elements, timbre is arguably the hardest to find words for. The timbre of a sound might be described as scratchy, smooth, ringing, hollow, piercing, rich, clanging, whispering, sparkling, breathy, harsh, resonant...and so on. Onomatopoeia is invaluable here; children can invent their own sound words. In fact, any kind of poetic description can help to get inside the sensation of different sound qualities. Timbre is so closely tied to the quality of how we physically perceive sound, with our whole bodies as sensors, that descriptions often draw on these physical responses too.

Duration: *the length of sounds, both their natural decay time and their length as patterned in the rhythmic aspects of music; the length of silences and rests; metre.*
Use words which help children to grasp the time-based aspect of sounds and of rhythms. These often borrow the mathematical vocabulary of time, number and measure. Movement words such as 'jumpy', 'swinging', 'marching' help to characterise rhythms based on particular groupings of note-lengths.

Single sounds can be compared and described as 'longer than' or 'shorter than' other sounds. Sounds may die away gradually or stop short; they may be 'damped' i.e. stopped before their natural end.

Musical rhythm may be based on a steady beat, with an underlying feeling of a regular pulse which may or may not be heard. Much rhythm vocabulary relates to the length of notes in music measured against a beat. The vocabulary of semibreves, minims, crotchets, quavers, semiquavers and 'dotted' notes is based entirely on durations measured as proportionally relative to a 'long' and its subsequent divisions into twos and threes. This vocabulary can be introduced as soon as it becomes meaningful. More simply, it might be useful to describe:

- the pulse; feeling the pulse;
- steady beats; no beat;
- rests or silent beats;
- beats divided in two or three;
- beats grouped in twos, threes, fours and fives; metre.

Discussion of metre and grouping of beats is often easiest initially in relation to familiar dance metres e.g. waltzes and minuets in threes, or by using headings derived from the 'style' settings on keyboards.

Notice that rhythm may also be free, with no regular beat at all. In this case, talk about how the music moves: freely, faster, slower and how silence is used.

Dynamics: *the drama of the sound; in particular the relative loudness or quietness of the music and the way this alters as the music develops; silence and accents.*
Use the words louder and quieter (avoiding softer which is possibly confusing) comparatively where possible, or qualify to try to be clear about the degree to which music is loud or quiet. It is common to talk about dynamic 'levels' and in some music dynamic changes are sudden, as if it had jumped from one level to another. Encourage children to heighten their awareness of the subtlety of dynamic effects and to feel these as related to other felt or dramatic or shaping forces in melody, rhythm, harmony and form. Accent, whilst belonging to the sphere of dynamics because of its relation to relative energy or force is intrinsically related to effects of rhythm and metre, so is often discussed in those contexts.

Silence often has a particular quality; it can be startling or restful according to context and it is useful to try to describe this too.

Pitch: *the highness or lowness of the music; the dimension in which melodies are shaped.*
Use words which use the metaphors of space and movement in space. Children find this one of the hardest areas to conceptualise and using the analogy of physical movement up and down in space seems to help, particularly if supported by visual representation as well. Standard musical notation uses the same convention, showing melodies as moving higher or lower on the stave. Again, high and low are best treated as comparative terms. Describing melodies calls for describing them as lines and shapes, and as moving by step or by jump, twisting and turning. The overall contour of a line might be described as jagged or smooth. The way we think of melody relates it to a mapping process in every sense. Part music and harmonic ideas are thought of in terms of vertical space, one part above another; chords are built of notes stacked up, happening simultaneously.

As note names are introduced, there is a choice between letter names i.e. A to G, with sharps (semitone higher) and flats (semitone lower) between, or the system which names positions on a scale relative to a moveable key note i.e. doh, re, mi etc. where doh can be any pitch.

Tempo: *the speed at which the music moves.*
Children easily confuse tempo or speed, which is measured against a beat, with aspects of duration. There can be a steady tempo i.e. a steady underlying beat, whilst rhythm patterns use increasingly shorter, and therefore faster sounding, notes. Use movement words to describe tempo as, for example, fast, lively, a walking pace, lazy, slow. Discuss small variations in rhythm against tempo, used expressively to pull back or push the music on, as well as music in which tempo increases or decreases gradually or makes definite changes.

Texture: *the quality produced by the number of layers in the music and how close together or far apart they are.*
Musical texture might be described as thick or thin, sparse or intricate. A texture might be a single line, single notes one at a time (monody); or it might be layered, with different parts moving together (homophonically) or at different times (polyphonically).

Lines might be closely woven together or spread out. An accompaniment might set a chordal texture underneath a melodic line. Pitch, timbre and rhythm as well as structure all contribute to musical texture.

Structure: *the overall shape of the music as a whole or within sections of it; how the music is built, musical form.*
Use words that describe how the music is put together: phrases, sections, repetitions of ideas, phrases or whole sections, or that refer to parts of it e.g. beginning, middle, end. Verse and chorus, call and response, are standard song structures. Structure can be thought of architecturally as how music is constructed, or as the drama of how music changes over time. As children's ability to grasp the larger time structures in music increases, vocabulary relating to forms of pieces such as rounds, canons, dance forms can be introduced. Discussion can also include words describing how music unfolds in time e.g. continuing, altering, developing, transforming, contrasting; these can be applied to timbre, texture and dynamics as well as to rhythmic, melodic and harmonic ideas.

It is wise to be wary of treating musical elements in isolation from each other. Although the above conceptual divisions may help to clarify the vocabulary associated with different elements, they have little justification in terms of trying to understand music in practice unless taken together, since they are interdependent and in many cases inseparable e.g. all melody has rhythm.

using language in musical contexts
From the musical point of view, language difficulties during the 7–11 age phase are most often caused by the straightforward lack of experience of talking and thinking about music in a musical context, that is, in relation to the immediate experiences of singing, playing and listening to music. This may be more than a dearth of opportunities for pupils to practise talking or writing themselves. Much more fundamentally it is often a lack of hearing adults talk – as composers, performers or critics, of reading writings about music, and of having conversations with a teacher who helps to 'scaffold' ways of talking or writing about music. All these act as examples; they model and enrich language use and give frameworks for talk in ways which simply offering vocabulary, naming, asking set questions and accepting or correcting answers to match, cannot do.

examples of talking and writing

This breadth of experience can easily be provided if resources are looked for from a variety of sources. For example:

- short quotations from artists are often included in CD notes; these can be read and discussed with children;
- newspaper and magazine articles and reviews provide very varied examples of comment on music, from artists themselves or from critics reviewing recordings or live events; short extracts can be chosen which demonstrate a particular kind of writing or talk, or that raise issues of relevance to children's work;
- recordings from radio or TV programmes can be used; two or three minutes from an interview or debate can supply excellent examples of how musicians view their work or how other people discuss it;
- biographical or autobiographical books as well as general texts about particular kinds of music, or even books of quotations, will supply examples of all kinds of different speech and writing; collecting extracts from these in individual notebooks or for a class display can help give a feel for the range of musical discourse;
- any adult who will visit and talk about music – their personal favourites, listening collection, or experiences with a local folk club, amateur operatic society or choir – can be an invaluable model of how we talk and think about music in our own lives;
- a visiting composer or performer who talks about their work can give another perspective which children can draw on; they can be asked to comment not just on the music but on what the artist had to say.

Taken together with the teacher's own input, contributions of these kinds greatly enhance children's awareness of the wider spectrum of musical experience and provide clear examples of how children themselves can begin to articulate their own musical descriptions, critiques, and responses. Examples of talking and writing can be discussed in terms both of the kind of talk about music which they represent and in terms of language styles of speaking and writing. By the end of this age-phase, children are well able to engage in this level of reflection and it can enhance their own language work enormously. For instance, examples might be categorised as:

- descriptions or analysis of the music itself, in musical language;
- descriptions of the music in more subjective, perhaps poetic, language;

- comment which relates music to its context e.g. of time, place or style, or to the composer or performer's intentions;
- descriptions of how the music makes the listener or performer feel, or what personal associations or images it evokes;
- talk about musical taste, likes and dislikes;
- evaluative judgments about how good or bad a piece or performance is.

Children can begin to distinguish the different language styles which go with pop and classical music criticism, for example, or with an encyclopaedia or CD-ROM entry as opposed to a CD sleeve or a book. Older pupils respond well to being asked explicitly to examine, compare and comment on other musicians' talk or writings about music. An awareness of permeating attitudes to gender, race and religion and an approach which seeks to give balanced representation can be key factors here in ensuring that children adopt similarly open approaches themselves and that individuals find enough models and endorsement to encourage them in their own linguistic expressions.

opportunities for talking and writing
Running alongside a rich environment of speech and writings about music is the need for varied opportunities for children to develop their own skills of using language in a musical context. Teachers can provide for this by making time and opportunity and by allowing for a variety of forms for expression, building on and extending the opportunities which arise all the time as part of composing, performing, listening and appraising.

- one child talks informally to the rest about their musical preferences, activities or listening collection; allow turns at this throughout the year; in aiming for informality and genuineness, rather than speech-making, this is usually best unprepared;
- one child interviews another or a visitor about a particular music topic or event; questions are prepared though not rigidly stuck to; a shortened *Desert Island Disc* format can be useful here;
- encourage children to introduce their work when presenting performances to the class or other audience; on a large-scale occasion they can prepare programme notes to go with these as well, researching examples for ideas about the kinds of things to say;
- make music notebook entries recording descriptions and reflections

on music composed or performed; choose occasions to do this when either the music is particularly memorable, or you have quite specific things to say; allow individuals some leeway in how often and to what extent they do this;

~ use a display space or class book for collecting individual contributions to writings about particular music listened to or under investigation; encourage children to opt to contribute a particular kind of writing e.g. some to research, some to review, some to give personal reactions, some to respond in poetry;

~ write cover notes for tapes of own performances or compositions which are then lodged in the classroom for individual listening on headphones; this can be linked to study of the kind of content and style used in published CD or cassette notes;

~ encourage individuals to write short contributions, articles, or letters to school wide publications (such as a one-off newsletter), or local newsletters or papers.

The important thing is that children are shown and taught and not just asked questions in a way that amounts to testing without preliminary input. Rich, lively, divergent talk interests children and their own ideas rapidly take off. Music can provide strong motivation for language work, particularly as children become more confident in their own musical individuality.

language and assessment
The language in which children are taught, the language in which they discuss musical activity and the language in which music learning and outcomes are assessed, whether by children or teachers, should be all of a piece.

music for voices

primary music: later years

This section looks at many aspects of making music with the voice in which children will be involved during the later years of primary schooling. Learning to sing a repertoire of standard songs and perform them well is a vitally important dimension of music education for children of this age. However, children will be involved not only in vocal performance but also in listening to and investigating songs and song singing of many styles and in making their own songs. Each aspect of children's voice work will integrate with, support and inform other aspects. So that, for example, listening to and investigating songs might supply ideas for composing songs and an understanding of song style in children's rehearsing of songs for performance. Or, similarly, improvising vocally and composing songs might lead to a deeper insight into songs being listened to or performed. This section presents ways of working in music for voices which broadens beyond the one strand of singing performance.

The section is organised in three parts. The first gives specific attention to the building of voice skills, the second to children's song-making and the third to developing two-voice work. While the first two parts take a specific focus, the third one offers a set of investigations in which an integrated approach blends listening, skill building, investigating and song-making. This third part is intended to give a set of suggestions and ideas in one area of vocal work: it does not aim to give fully planned units of work. Songs are included, chosen to represent a range of repertoire.

individual voices

A class of children is made up of thirty individual singers, each child with their own unique sound, each child at a different stage of singing development, each with different enthusiasms and interests in vocal music. Only differentiated approaches to singing can cater for such individualities and offer to every child the opportunity both to make the most of their own vocal potential and to develop their own vocal identity. Similarly, children's development as song-writers depends to a large extent on the scope they are given to work to their own strengths and interests, bringing together their creative work in language and music.

Starting with the idea that children are first and foremost individual singers and only join voices with others for musical reasons or for pedagogical reasons, is a very different starting point from that which takes all school singing to be of the large-group kind and anything else an unusual deviation. The idea of children all working individually on vocal work might seem impractical, alarming even, but behind lies the importance of recognising individual learning pathways and making room for these in the way vocal work is organised.

If they are to make good progress in developing their vocal work, many children will need specific help, tailored to their particular needs. Differentiated teaching is, after all, the norm in every other area of the curriculum. No one would assume that all children learning to read can be taught as a crowd, each is given books and support designed to match their current ability. A singing recovery group, for example, might give extra help to some identified as in need. Such approaches signal to children that singing is something for which there are serious expectations of achievement. All this assumes that throughout the years of upper primary schooling teachers will take careful notice of and track each child's progress.

Similarly, children's development as song-writers depends to a large extent on the scope they are given to work individually on their own material. Such experience enables them to develop their personal skills and inventiveness as well as a sense of their own compositional pathway. This enables children to work to their own strengths and interests, bringing together creative ideas in language and music. The class as a whole benefit from hearing the wide range of songs produced by individual children and the differences between each composer.

On another level, differentiating for individual voices is about creating opportunities for children to develop lines of personal interest. This is vital if children are to develop an individual identity as a singer. If singing all together as a class or school and singing pre-selected repertoire is the only kind of vocal experience on offer this can be limiting. For ten and eleven year olds in-school singing repertoire can begin to sound increasingly outdated and uninteresting while songs heard outside school are enticing and have relevance. Large group singing to bring community together is, for better or worse, much less a part of our changing society. Children's dominant experiences are of seeing and listening to solo or small group singers in the media who present a highly individual style and repertoire. While not suggesting that community singing experiences which have an important place in classroom and school life should be abandoned, widening the kinds of vocal activities which are provided will give children more scope to develop their own lines of interest – with the bonus that this is likely to allow connections to be made between vocal music in school and beyond.

What follows are two suggestions as to how vocal work can be planned for in the classroom which will make more room for individual pathways of working to weave in and out of other whole class or large group singing experiences.

class song book

A class song book can contain songs from many different sources collected by the children and teacher over the year. There might be favourite songs contributed by individual children or songs from home and family brought in after a song-search set as a homework task. The book can include songs composed by children alongside those composed by others together with a repertoire of traditional songs. Seasonal songs, following the annual calendar of festivals and ceremonies, will also have their place in the songbook. The teacher adds new songs which are planned for the class or individuals to learn during the coming term or year – they might be added to the song book with challenges, instructions and information: 'Here is a song which has a very difficult melody shape; it is an old Scottish song – perhaps someone will be able to begin working out the tune on the keyboard before I sing it to you'.

The songs can be collected in many different media: written song words, notated versions (hand-written or computer produced), recordings on cassette, CD or video. Recordings may be made by children, teacher, other adults or commercially produced. Annotations remind songbook readers who gave the song, where it came from originally (if the contributor knows this), who knows the song well and can teach it to you. They will include any special instructions about the performance of the song in keeping with its style, if certain movements or dances should accompany the song, if it is only for singing at certain times or in certain places, and so on.

The song book belongs to the class. It is a reference book, an aide-memoire and captures something personal about each of the contributors. Set out in the book area or music area, children can look through and sing from the song book or listen to recordings as they wish. At class singing times choices can be made from the book, either for everyone to sing together or for individuals or groups to sing for an audience of other children. As they move on to a new class, the song book can be taken as a starting point for the next teacher and a reference book for repertoire covered.

circle time for voice work

Every week or two weeks the class assemble for a session at which ongoing vocal work from individual, pairs or groups of children is gathered. There might be song compositions in progress, language, song and drama projects, composed songs in the process of learning and rehearsing, investigations into song singing from recordings or song notation tasks. The children can present their work, discuss their progress and air any particular difficulties. Self-assessment, promoted in this kind of discussion, is important in developing children's independence as singers. The teacher responds with feedback, and in this way can engage all the children in thinking through ideas or problems which the work of just one child has raised.

This working format gives the teacher an opportunity to keep track of work in progress and decide with the children what they could move on to next. This might be a time to keep the music notebook up to date. On one page the children keep a record of song repertoire listened to and performed and add comments on how their singing is progressing. The notebook provides an ongoing record of voice work for each child, and can include ideas and sketches for songs used as part of the composing process. From this information the teacher can compile a separate, quick-glance tick sheet that gives an overview of all children's work. Significant examples of children's work might be kept in written version, recorded on tape or video.

voice skills

The seven to eleven age phase, as children mature physically, is an important time for the development of singing skills. Scanning the whole age phase, there might be seven year olds who arrive in September having only achieved the first steps of singing competence, just able to control the pitching of their voices to join in with songs which have simple melodies. At the other end of the age phase are eleven year olds with developed vocal skills, perhaps having had specialist lessons in singing as choristers, musical show singers or children's choir members. Catering for such a wide band of skill levels and ensuring progression and continuity is built in to teaching at all levels presents a challenge to teachers.

If each child is to develop their vocal potential progressively through these years of upper primary schooling, voice skills need to be worked at seriously. Learning to use voices well is not a natural result of simply taking part in lots of singing along with everyone else nor something which is linked to maturity, automatically improving as children grow older. Nor is singing ability gifted to some and not to others; each child can develop their singing voice through carefully managed opportunities to develop listening awareness and voice skills.

During these years children can acquire good singing habits. What is more important, with raised skill levels, they have the chance to gain a lasting and positive sense of themselves as singers. As children move from first years to later years of singing they are capable of widening the pitch range of their voices and of learning to control voice pitching across that widened range so that they can sing songs with more complex melodic shapes. They will be able to learn to match their voice pitching to the singing of others more successfully than in the first years of singing so that duo, ensemble and choir singing has increased possibilities. Physically they can learn to improve posture, control of breathing and how they use the parts of the mouth so that technical skills develop. They can come to know a wider variety of kinds of song in many different styles and some of the more specific voice techniques associated with certain styles. Voice changes caused by the onset of puberty in both girls and boys may occur in a small number of children. It is important for the teacher working with eleven year olds in the very last stages of primary school to be alert to physiological changes which may cause some children to have difficulty reaching certain pitch ranges and to sing with a breathier quality to the voice (Cooksey and Welch, 1997).

The voice and parts of the body used in singing need to be warmed and loosened before singing – just as in any physical activity, the warm-up is essential to avoid strain and possible damage. Encouraging children to notice and think about how the voice and singing body feel, as well as how they sound, is important for voice health. As in all musical skill learning, listening is central, so that as the children make physical adjustments they become associated with a listening search for just the best sound. Children will build an understanding of good vocal technique if the purpose and physical detail of each vocal skill activity are explained to them. The skill activities are isolated here in the list which follows, but in practice it is crucial that these relate to and are applied in musical experiences.

A set of first activities for vocal skills is suggested in *Music in the Early Years* (Young and Glover, 1998). The following list provides both a resumé and further advice.

activities

body-ready?

Some first exercises:

- Stretch both arms upwards, push up right and left arm alternately several times.
- Flop over loosely from the waist, allowing both arms to hang 'rag-doll'. Straighten the back gradually to an upright standing position.
- Rotate the shoulders, one way then the other.
- Tip the head very gently from side to side.

For posture:
Standing is preferable to sitting, and sitting on a chair far preferable to a floor-sitting cross-legged slouch.

- Stand tall, with feet slightly apart, weight well balanced and a little forward over the balls of the feet.
- Set the shoulders back and down. *This raises the rib cage and increases the volume of air in the lungs.*
- Allow the hands to hang loosely down by the sides.
- Keep the head well positioned at the top of the spine, feel that a 'thread' at the top of the head draws it upward.
- Widen and lengthen the torso.

breathing-ready?

- Breathe low in the chest, filling the lower, abdominal part and not high in the chest. *Children will find this kind of breathing by lying flat on the floor and feeling their stomachs gently rise and fall.*
- Breathe in quickly as if surprised. Notice the sudden expansion of the diaphragm.
- Stand and lean over, place hands around the waist and notice the expansion at the waist when air is breathed in.
- Blow all the air out of the lungs in a continuous, controlled stream of air.
- Practise 'panting' for breath control. Draw air in slowly as if sucking through a straw and breathe out slowly.

voice-ready?

Open throat:

- Open and relax throat, as if about to yawn.
- Imagine how the throat feels just before taking a drink or when suddenly amazed.
- Vocalise 'oo' and 'aah' sounds to loosen the throat.

Mouth parts:

- Massage the cheeks to loosen up the facial muscles for singing.
- Use lips, tongue generously to pronounce words and produce crisp consonants.
- Drop the lower jaw, 'hangdog' style to relax the jaw. *Just opening the mouth wide and stretching is less helpful.*

Singing Tone:

- Speak the five long vowel sounds, ee, ay, ah, oh, oo. *Vowel sounds colour the tone and so forming vowel sounds well is essential for good singing.*
- Sing slide the vowel sound aah and oo on a downward glissando after breathing in gently.
- Sing the five long vowel sounds on a single note, nee, nay, nah, noh, noo.

Prepare the singing of this song, an American spiritual: *'Body-ready?' 'Breathing-ready?' 'Voice-ready?'*

voice skills: amen

The smooth melody of this song needs to be supported and sustained by correct breathing. A breath can be taken at the end of the first two short phrases where there are rests. The final longer phrase will be sung through ideally on one breath and this will need practice, particularly if a fairly slow tempo is chosen. At the same time, work to find a good singing tone. Sing the vowel sound of the 'a' of amen 'English accent' as an 'aah' with the jaw loose and relaxed and listen for a full and resonant vocal tone. Then try 'American accent style' with the short 'ay' vowel sound and listen for the difference in tone. Sustaining and sliding clear vowel sounds over three notes of the melody in the first two phrases is difficult and this will also need to be singled out for practice. Singing short portions of the melody to the different vowel sounds – oo, ee with a starting consonant – will give further practice at producing a rich vocal tone.

The children can experiment with moving the song around in their own vocal register and find where it sits most comfortably for them. They could do this in their individual practice of this song.

extending voice techniques

In the early years, children will probably be singing with an unforced singing sound producing the distinctive timbre and tone of young children's voices. As they get older, children are hearing vocal music of many different kinds which exploits a wide range of techniques, timbres and styles and they will become interested in this wider variety. They are already good imitators of much of the vocal music they hear, as any eavesdropping on playground pop song routines will soon tell. So, alongside developing the individuality of their voice, children listen for, recognise, experiment and learn the performance skills associated with some of these extended vocal techniques.

Vocal music, world wide, has developed vocal techniques in directions quite different to the usual singing voices common to Western classical traditions. There are some published collections, for example, Voices of the World, an Anthology of Vocal Expression (CMX 374 1010.12) which is a wonderful sampler of the variety and diversity of singing traditions. Schools can build their own collections. In addition, performers and composers of contemporary art music since the 1950s have developed extended vocal techniques in their work. Pop styles and jazz have pushed the boundaries of vocal music in other directions.

Timbre almost more than anything else marks out a music as folk, jazz, pop, opera, South Asian and so on. Just listening for the timbre is enough for most of us to place a song geographically, stylistically, historically. Making a distinctive singing sound is crucially part of vocal skill – the way breathing, mouth parts, resonances of body cavities are used to produce the vocal sound. For one thing, describing vocal timbre in words poses difficulties. Words can be chosen to describe how the sound has been produced physically – as guttural, throaty, chesty, nasal, or to associate it with other sounds, such as whining, growling, husky, hooting, etc. But in the end words fall short and simply listening to lots of music from different traditions, learning about vocal technique and working to reproduce the vocal sounds is the way children will build a repertoire of vocal timbre for their own work. Singers with special knowledge of certain styles and of how, technically, the voice sound is produced – a Somerset folk singer, an opera singer, for example – can give specialised instruction in workshop sessions offered by professional outreach or community music organisations.

Some examples of extended vocal techniques are given below together with suggestions of vocal performers whose recordings could become a focus for listening and investigating. Teachers' personal collections of music will contain many other examples of singing performance which could equally well be used.

falsetto:
Singing in an unnaturally high voice.
Listen to:
- The Bee Gees: *The Very Best of the Bee Gees* (Polydor 847 339 2)
- Kate Bush: *The Whole Story* (EMI 7464142)

gravel voice:
A rough, husky voice common in blues, jazz and rock.
Listen to:
- Tina Turner: *Simply the Best* (CPD 79 6630 2)
- Louis Armstrong: *Louis Armstrong: Greatest Hits* (Curb Records CB 701)

shouting, calling voice:
Styles developed to carry the voice far as in singing for outdoor spaces, yodelling, or above a loud background as in heavy metal music where a shouting style of singing is common.
Listen to:
- Reef: *Glow* (CB 791)
- Bulgarian State Television Female Choir: *Ritual: Les Mystere Des Voix Bulgares* (Elektra Nonesuch, Explorer Series 7559-79349)
In Bulgarian style, the voice is sometimes called a 'hey' voice – a particular technique of projecting the sound.
- Adzido, Pan African Dance ensemble: *Dance and Song from South Africa* (Siye, Goli EUCD 1223)

chanting, rapping:
The speaking voice and singing voice blend across chanting and rapping styles.

Listen to:
- Sweet Honey in the Rock: 'Young and Positive' Tr. 8, *I Got Shoes* (9 42534 2)
- Meredith Monk: *The Tale* in *The Education of the Girl Child*

whispers, sighs, breathy sounds:
The sound of breathing in and out may be used for musical purposes, perhaps as a special timbre or to add rhythmic effects.
Listen to:
- Inuit Throat Games: Tr. 13, *Voices of the World* (CMX 374 1010 12)
- Cranberries: 'No need to argue' Tr. 5, *Empty* (Island CID 8029)

vibrato:
Adding vibrato to the voice is a kind of decorative style. In western operatic style singers apply considerable vibrato to their voices to increase the volume and resonance of their voices.
Listen to:
- Celia Cruz: *Queen of Cuban Rhythm* (MCCD 220)
- Jessye Norman: *The Very Best of Jessye Norman* (Philips 454 693-2)

ornamentation:
Ornamentation is one of the crucial musical characteristics which defines a musical style. Singers add trills, extra notes, turns and slides to decorate the melodic line.
Listen to:
- Fado singers from Portugal: *The Story of Fado* (EMI 7243)
- Marta Sebestyen: *The best of Marta Sebestyen* (LC 7433)
- Vijay, (lead singer for Achanak): Tr. 1, 6, 12,13, *East 2 West: Bhangra for the Masses* (Music Club/Nachural Records MCCD 121)
- Nusrat Fateh Ali Khan: *Mustt Mustt:* (Realworld 0777 7862212 3) A Pakistani singer of Qawwali – the devotional music of the Sufis.

melisma:
One syllable of a word which slides over a string of different notes.
Listen to:
- Sequentia: *Canticles of Ecstasy Hildegard of Bingen* (DHM 05472 77320 2) or

- Monks of Silos Abbey: *Canto Gregoriano*
- Dougie MacLean: *The Dougie MacLean Collection* (Putumayo World Music M117–2)
- Mariah Carey: *Music Box* (Columbia 474270 2)

song writing

Offering song writing opportunities which run alongside the above kind of detailed attention to voice skills and different stylistic ways of producing the voice works to the benefit of each. For most children, the main tool in song-making will be their own voice. As they become more skilled in using it and extend their repertoire of vocal styles and techniques, their song writing will be enriched accordingly. Conversely, the detailed and repetitive work involved in composing songs brings with it opportunities to build confidence and skills in performing vocally. Many children sing solo or in a small group willingly and almost without thinking when the song is of their own making whilst being far more reluctant to perform learnt songs in this way. In situations where older children have, for whatever reasons, become resistant to singing, a song writing project can be an excellent way of revitalising their interest and breaking down prejudices.

Almost any opportunity for creative writing can be an opportunity for song writing. Building on early years experience of spontaneous, improvised song-making and very simple composed and memorised songs, by the age of 7 or 8 most children are well able to start developing songwriting as a genuine medium of personal expression alongside other text based forms such as poetry and story writing. Even where song making comes as a completely new activity, it does not take long, given encouragement, for children to launch themselves into this sphere of composition and to make rapid progress.

One reason for this is undoubtedly the enormous part songs play in any and every musical culture. This is the one musical form which is most unlikely to be unfamiliar to any child. The pop world alone, offers a constantly changing parade of singers and singer-songwriters presenting single songs and more sustained collections across a huge range of styles and types of performance. Characters in children's films and stories break into song at all kinds of moments. World folk traditions contain another whole tranche of song formats and performance styles. And many children will have direct experience of live song singing from one source or another. This all combines to provide plenty of images of how a song finishes up – what it's like, when it's sung, and the kinds of things singers and writers say about their songs. This gives children as composers a clear context in which to work, whatever the hazards of the particular styles they've encountered.

More practically, song writing is probably the easiest form of composition to organise, since it requires almost no resources and much of it can be managed either as homework, or with children sitting in their own places at ordinary tables, thinking and humming or singing to themselves, jotting down ideas or using a tape recorder or Dictaphone, by themselves. Flexibility about time, about when and for how long work can be carried out, does, however, tend to improve the quality of songs produced. Some anticipation that song composition will progress in stages, just as a piece of writing will, helps to increase expectations and also enjoyment. Standards drop when children are expected to compose something quickly in ten minutes at the end of a day on a given subject all at the same time.

There is no reason why song writing should be a synchronised activity, nor why the whole class need undertake the same projects. If approached as part of an individual folio of language and/or music activity, pupils can choose different occasions on which to write songs alongside other kinds of writing. If linked to particular events or times of year, one or two children only can contribute on each occasion. Songs may be used in conjunction with almost any curriculum area, offered as free-standing expressions, or for particular use e.g. in an assembly, for listening at the end of a day, and so on. Individual pupils can choose the context and opportunity which interests them most. Within a school year choices might be drawn from:

- topics of personal interest or significance: *beliefs and feelings, family events, stories, favourite pets;*
- standard song forms: *lullabies, ballads, work songs, nonsense songs, protest songs;*

- issues arising in school or beyond: *environmental issues, relationships, bullying; thoughtful songs, assembly songs;*
- topics from history: *recording or commenting on events as first person, 'eye-witness' or family relative, telling a story, raising an issue;*
- seasonal topics and special events: *seasons, festivals, celebrations, visits, endings and goodbyes;*
- songs for dramatic performance: *assemblies, shows, informal class dramas.*

Children may also decide to compose a song specifically to try out a particular voice technique, such as those introduced above, or song form e.g. verse and chorus. Ideas may come after listening to a song or style of song which particularly appeals and individuals can take these on for further exploration themselves. Two or three quality pieces of song-writing by each child each year across the age phase adds up to a substantial collection and is infinitely preferable to more frequent activities lacking depth or scope for real commitment. All that is needed to set the work going is that the teacher establishes a general approach which incorporates song composition into the normal spectrum of creative opportunities.

starting song-writing

Deciding how to start work with a class completely unused to song writing will depend on children's age and attitudes and how the teacher wants to work this activity into the wider class picture. Brenda Kirwan, working with a class of 29 7–11year olds in a fairly cramped rural school, describes how she began at the beginning of the half-term break simply by asking everybody to *'have a go at writing a song of any sort you like, about anything you like, and bring it back to school where you can record it'*. To her surprise, although there were some groans of 'I don't know how', the first songs came back within a week and by the end of term she had a song from nearly everyone in the class (Kirwan, 1997). The strength of this approach is that the work brought back gives both teacher and children insight into the compositional issues, the difficulties, and the possibilities. The teacher immediately has a set of starting points for further input, which is well differentiated and closely related to children's needs. Pupils have the motivation of having made a start and found, often to their surprise, that they can make a song for themselves. Hearing each others' work also boosts interest and this establishes a community of composers within which work towards developing skills and techniques has a clear context and rationale.

If the teacher's preference is for more gradual ways of moving into song-writing, the following may be more appropriate starting points:

activities

~ focus some writing work on song lyrics of a particular kind e.g. folk ballads, songs about a local character or heroine: study lots of examples and ask pupils to write lyrics of their own, bearing in mind aspects of structure, word rhythms, refrains; offer the option for some pupils to set the words to music once written;

~ draw attention to features of a song currently being learnt; ask if anyone would like to try these out in a song of their own;

~ commission a song for a particular occasion; discuss requirements, e.g. how long it should be, what the performance situation will be, the capabilities of the singer(s), whether there is to be accompaniment or not; agree who will take the commission on and give a deadline date for finishing; make progress checks at appropriate intervals but give help only if requested;

~ include song-making as an option alongside a writing project aimed at younger children as an audience: instead of writing a story to be read to Y1 or 2, make a song to sing to or with them, or include a song in your story.

These starting points all carry with them assumptions that pupils can and will be able to come up with songs given purpose and opportunity. Establishing this is the first step. Teachers can be tempted to think that they must teach children how to write a song before asking them to do it. But this is to misunderstand both the learning and the song writing process. There is no 'how to write a song' since there is no standard song, nor standard writing process, and compositional decisions about which rhythms, tune, structure, treatment of words etc. have always to be made uniquely in each particular instance. Learning to write songs is therefore a long-term process made up of the individual writing song after song and learning from each. This does not imply, however, that there is no role for the teacher. On the contrary, specific inputs to help pupils develop technique, understanding and a sense of their own direction is vital. But it is crucial that such teaching runs alongside practice, since it cannot effectively precede it. This is because, ideally, teaching input will always take its cue from issues raised by the child's own work, and techniques will be developed as the need for them arises. Otherwise progress is far too slow and much time wasted imparting techniques which have already been grasped aurally, or which have no present meaning for the child.

developing song-writing

The key role for the teacher in developing children's song writing is the role of a listener who can reflect back to the child how the song is heard, what structures are apparent, how the music changes as it goes on, how words and music interrelate, and also, subjectively, what the impact of the music is. The skills in doing this are mainly observational and analytical; making judgments has very little part to play since composers must do this for themselves. It is also useful to bear in mind that offering description helps to extend children's musical perception in a way that simply questioning cannot. Particularly with younger children, there is also an element of memorising and helping to 'play back' the music, giving a sense of its overall shape, not easy to grasp in a time-based art. The aim of all these strategies is to raise the child's awareness of what they have done in the music and to offer the perspective of a new listener who comes fresh to the work. The latter is the 'audience' element which is invaluable for the process of developing any creative work.

For the teacher, the listening role has two aspects to it:
● listening to the song as music in its own right;
● listening for what the song indicates about the child's creativity, skills and understanding in relation to song writing.

Bringing these together, and taking into account a wider knowledge of the child's stage of development and learning needs gives the basis on which the teacher can decide what to say and how to respond to the work. There are some occasions when just listening is enough. Beyond these, if the time is judged to be right the teacher can:
● give an overview of the song's type, structure, or style;

- draw attention to one or more detailed aspects of words, melody, rhythm, phrasing, naming or describing the devices used;
- give a personal response (not evaluation) to the mood or feeling of the piece, or to its dramatic impact;
- make connections which locate the work in relation to other songs performed or heard, or particular song styles or types.

This may sound quite a challenge when considered in the abstract, but as soon as children bring work to be listened to, actual examples usually raise fairly clear talking points and learning issues of their own.

Just as important as offering a listener's perspective is that the teacher encourages each child to reflect on and talk about their own work along similar lines. Once again, focusing on how the song is and on understanding the detail of how it is put together and the effects which result is the main agenda. To begin with speculative questions, for example about how the music could be better, is to lose almost all the learning value of coming to a depth of understanding about what is 'in' the piece as it is. Staying with the work, thinking through its issues, pinpointing new skills which are shown to be needed and then planning a next step or a next piece is much more profitable than thinking about how this piece might have been. This kind of reflection and analysis can be carried out initially with the whole class looking at a few examples of songs written by individuals.

> The class listened to and discussed the first five songs produced by individual members of the class. They identified the following list of song features for consideration:
> - tune, words and rhythm: any or all of these can be repeated;
> - songs can be in verses, songs can have verses and choruses;
> - different speeds can be used to give different moods in different kinds of songs;
> - tune and words might match e.g. the tune going up for words describing going up;
> - major and minor keys (recognised by some, appreciated by all as 'different type of sound') can affect mood;
> - songs have shape: some described as 'zig-zags' or 'triangles' depending on the way the tunes went;

- beginnings of songs often have a tune that goes up;
- endings of songs often have a tune that goes down, slows up, dies down/fades, or holds onto a long note;
- songs often begin and end on the same note;
- some songs sound like other songs.

(adapted from Kirwan, 1997)

This catalogue of observations shows how quickly a small number of examples can open up an agenda for investigation that could take children on towards a much more sophisticated awareness of what compositional choices they have and the consequences of making them. The features noted can be explored further using listening examples from a variety of sources; some can be treated as hypotheses and tested against the class song book repertoire; others can form the focus for additional theoretical explanation; and they can become features which a next song composition sets out to exploit more fully. So, having listened to and discussed examples of children's work, there will be topics or skills which can be identified as needing further teacher input or instruction and work can continue from there.

Finally, children, like most composers, cannot work in isolation. A set of strategies is needed which will promote a rich and stimulating context for song writing and bring a sense of contact with other composers and with different methods of working. These might include:

- a teacher, carer, or friend modelling song writing with the class – thinking aloud, trying out possibilities, building up a song gradually, drafting, editing and preparing for performance;
- a visiting singer-songwriter talking about his/her ways of working and performing examples; children can prepare questions and interview the visitor (Kerr, 1997);
- using class song book or recorded listening repertoire to discuss song-making from the composer's point of view, speculating if necessary e.g. *'Which part of the song do you think was composed first?' 'What do you think the composer was thinking about most in making this song?'*
- researching what song composers have said or written about the processes of composing; this can be done through newspapers, magazines, CD covers, and TV interviews, as well as books. e.g.

Annie Lennox: 'sometimes you just have to force yourself to sit down and face a blank page' (Randal, 1996).

moving into part singing

The third part of this section on music for voices looks closely at part singing from its absolute beginnings through to first partsongs.

planning points

Moving from single-line, unison singing to singing songs in which two or more parts are combined represents a huge leap for children, one which teachers sometimes rush ambitiously. It is worth remembering that learning to sing in parts does not represent a 'benchmark' in a stage by stage progression of learning to perform songs but alternatively represents a broadening of voice music work into another dimension. Working with single line songs in solo or unison singing will continue to be an important and developing strand of music with the voice. Similarly, songs of more than one part do not represent, historically or culturally, some higher level of musical achievement than unison songs.

This series of investigations suggests small, progressive steps for moving into part singing and looks at the learning involved. The starting points for these investigations are varied to illustrate the way in which voice work will integrate listening, investigating, improvising, composing and performing. The starting points include:

- children's improvised vocal work;
- children's improvisations using a known song as the starting point;
- learning a set song and performing it;
- vocal activities designed to introduce one aspect of part singing;
- listening to a recording of the singing of others;
- listening to a recording and joining with singing one voice part;
- listening to a recording as a way of learning the song and performing with the recording as backing;
- studying a score.

And from these starting points the investigations are organised into four parts:
- vocal improvising with a partner;
- singing the same melody in turns;
- adding a layer to the melody;
- singing two different melodic lines together.

vocal improvising with a partner

When two get together to sing, there are an infinite number of ways in which voices can blend or bump into one another to create different effects of two sounds in harmony. The interaction of two voices with one another, taking turns, or singing at the same time, one voice as lead and the other as follower, interweaving, moving in similar directions or in opposition produces ever-interesting musical structures.

Children's part singing will progress on the one hand from improvised activities in which they explore, try out and develop a confidence to follow their own imaginations and on the other hand from a teaching approach which focuses their attention upon the small detail of pitch relationships between voices and demands skills, refinement and precision. Both sides move forward together, carefully dovetailed. Some preparatory work with two voices might include the following activities for voice work with a partner which aim to encourage both listening awareness and a freedom to improvise vocally:

- Sing a long sound on one single pitch. A partner must join in with exactly the same note. Can the two voices match exactly? Pairs of children help one another by listening. Match can involve not just pitch, but same vowel sounds, timbre and equal dynamics.
- Sing a long sound on one single pitch and a partner joins in with the same note, then moves away to a new sound and then back again, then sings a pitch slide which moves away further and back. Can the first note holder keep the same pitch throughout?
- Slide the voice slowly from high to low on a vowel sound (aah, oo). A partner slides the voice from low to high. Sing opposite directions at the same time. Sit opposite one another, look and listen. Each traces the voice direction with a finger in the air – the co-ordination involved makes this more difficult. Extend this activity into a game of

aeroplane wings (stand or sit opposite with arms outstretched to side) which follow the rise and fall of the voices.

~ Sing a voice sliding pathway that swoops up and down – not too fast. With a partner improvise two different pathways. If possible end on the same note. Draw two pathways on paper, trace with a finger and sing together.

In all these activities the children are encouraged to listen to and discuss the kind of effects produced by the two part singing. What directions did the voices move in, what effects did they produce? It is valuable to invite pairs of children to be listening partners to other pairs of children and to give comments. Visualising pitch directions with movements or drawings helps to fix aural perception.

| notice |

Those children who are able to use their voices across a wide pitch range and improvise freely. Listen carefully for those who show a particular ability to create interesting and pleasing melodic lines.

Some may still have difficulty with controlling the pitch of their voices – both the precise holding of certain pitches and the freedom to slide and glide their voices in many directions will be beneficial. Until children gain in voice pitching skills, moving into independent two-part voice work may pose particular difficulties.

To move methodically into part singing has all-round benefits for children's vocal work. Voice pitching skills are developed more precisely when children learn to hear their own singing in relation to another voice. When a child sings along with another singer they must be able to track two sources of singing, their own and that of their partner. The child's own singing rings and vibrates internally, in the body, as well as being heard externally as if coming from a source outside of themselves. The partner's singing arrives from a second external source. So, the task is one of 'double-listening' in which two quite different 'sound fields' must be monitored simultaneously. It is important to have clearly in mind that singing well, particularly when singing with others in unison or in parts, depends on aural skills which can track more than one thing at a time and not, as is commonly thought, in being able to hold your own in competition with another voice which must be aurally 'blocked out'.

Developing this two-sided listening is a primary task. A good way to start is to encourage one child to sing very quietly something confidently known. The teacher quietly sings a drone note or a simple ostinato part with the child's singing and then asks: *as you were singing, what did you hear me sing? Listen again. Can you hear?* This kind of activity can take place in a class circle with other children listening in carefully. Because learning to sing well depends upon aural awareness, it can be developed equally well through activities in which children are not actively singing but actively listening.

singing in turns

Turn-taking is a good way for children to become used to some of the skills involved in part singing. It creates two singing parts which follow one another, sequenced in time, rather than parts which are layered, sounding simultaneously in time. Turn-taking accustoms children to the idea of having two singers who work together but take different tasks and encourages them to listen and track another part in order to judge when, or when not to sing. It is also a good way of developing internal hearing because it encourages children to run the whole song in their heads stitching together their silent and sung portions as one.

Paired, children can work with known songs to find ways of turn-taking to make interesting and effective performances. Children can go on to use the different kinds of turn-by-turn structures they discover in their individual song composing work.

call and response

Call and response songs are singing dialogues. Turn-taking between a lead singer who 'calls' and another singer or group of singers who reply is the very essence of the song's structure. The response may be very short, little more than a shout or two in reply, it may be an exact echo of the leader's part or it may be a short phrase which complements. In some songs, if the response is quite long, the lead singer may start again before the response is finished creating an overlapping effect.

This song echoes exactly. With its limited pitch range it is suitable for those who are not yet pitching their voices securely or a group of new Year 3 children. Encourage individual children to take the lead singing role and to vary the way they sing – sometimes loud, quiet, fast, slow, with accentuated notes and different kinds of voices.

fills or 'breaks'

A fill is a short add-on sung at the end of the phrase to cover a pause in the flow of the music and to connect two phrases or sections. Fills may be fixed but are often improvised – an ornamentation of the last note or an echo of the melodic motif just heard. In this spiritual one child sings the main melody while another 'fills' either with improvised 'alleluys' at the end of each phrase or an echo of 'at your door'.

The 'fill' should not be attempted until the song is well absorbed. The main melody singer must be sure to sustain the final note of each phrase to provide the lower harmony note. A good way to work on this song is to make a recorded version of the song with which children can practise singing their end of phrase additions – karaoke style. The short snatches of melody for the fills will emerge from an instinctive feel for the harmony of the song, so re-hearings and practice time are important. Eventually two or more singers can prepare a performance as lead singer with backing.

...AT YOUR DOOR!

Some-bo-dy's kno-cking at your door, _____

...AT YOUR DOOR!

Some-bo-dy's kno-cking at your door, _____

O ____ sin- ner, why don't you ans- wer?

...AT YOUR DOOR!

Some-bo - dy's kno-cking at your door. _____

hocketting

Hocket derives from the French hoquet (hiccup). Single notes or a few notes are sung or played in turns. Passages in hocket are frequently found in thirteenth and fourteenth century vocal or instrumental music. They were always fast and the effect of hocketting was to liven the texture. Children can be helped to understand the technique by listening to a small, delicate song of the Mbenzele people from the Central African Republic (track 28, *Voices of the World*) where a singer alternates pipe sounds with voice sounds; the effect is quite transparent. A song in similar style of half-singing, half-playing could be improvised easily with recorders, ocarinas or whistle.

activity

↜ Hocketting makes an excellent game for voice pitching skills. Children sing one note each in turn of a song they know well. This works best if the song is fairly slow in tempo and simple in rhythm – try singing the round on page 62 as a hocket. However skilfully done, the effect is always slightly uneven and hesitant.

notice

Those children who can turn-take in singing with a partner. Are they able to lead or respond as appropriate? Do they listen carefully to the singing of their partner and try to match their own voice, its pitch, dynamic level, timbre, the speed at which they sing, to what they hear?

singing an added layer to a melody

This section moves on to singing an added part to accompany a melody. The added layer might be a continuous single note, a drone, or a short repetitive musical idea, an ostinato, providing a stable background against which the melody is heard. The interest arises from the contrast between the melody and its background, the way in which pitch relationships are created which blend or pull at one another. Very often the added layer is sung at a lower pitch, creating a kind of ground level sound upon which the melody builds, but drone notes and ostinati patterns can sound wonderful if sung within and around, tangled in the melody line or rising above it.

activity

drones

↜ In the vocal activities in the earlier section 'vocal improvising with a partner' it was suggested that one child could sing on one pitch continuously while their partner sings sliding pitch shapes against the held note (see page 53). Move on from this activity to suggest that the wandering voice shifts very slowly from note to note – if it helps a conductor can guide the voice movement with hand gestures. Listen acutely for the effects of note against note as one melody line moves away from the drone sound and for the magic moment when both voices finally settle back onto the same pitch.

The value of this kind of activity is in encouraging children to be comfortable with improvising freely with their voices and at the same time develop listening awareness for the detail of just one note sounding against another.

A next stage might be to sing a drone note through known songs – to find out how this sounds. The drone note is usually sung more comfortably and effectively to the song words or short phrases of words lifted from the song, or made up syllable sounds – a single 'la' sound is more difficult to sustain and inclined to lose the pitch. (If this is a real difficulty, instruments can join with voices in playing the drone.) A week's task might be to revisit all kinds of known song melodies and experiment with singing the melodies against a single drone note. A list of the songs and comments about the results can be made in notebooks – science experiment style. The starting note of the song will probably (although not always) suggest the pitch of the drone note. Listen to the results and discover all the weird and wonderful effects which might be produced. Perceptive listening is vital to begin to absorb just how the drone is working with and against the melody.

Here is a Hebridean traditional song which sounds effective with an added 'bag-pipe' drone on just a single note, best sung to syllable sounds which emphasise the pulse, or some kind of short repetitive musical idea which evolves from the drone. The note a fifth higher can be slotted in sometimes, it fits in quite smoothly. Snatches of song words can suggest rhythmic patterns for drone singing.

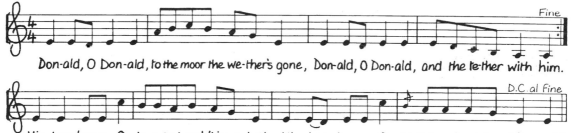

Don-ald, O Don-ald, to the moor the we-ther's gone, Don-ald, O Don-ald, and the te-ther with him.

Hin, han, hur-ry O, Is-a-bel and 'Liz-a-beth, Hin, han, hur-ry O, McCal-um's girl and Don-ald.

The Gaelic is:

Dhomhnuill, a Dhomhnuill	Hinn, hainn hurra bhi!
Thug am molt am monadh air!	Isabeil is Ealasaid:
Dhomhnuill, a Dhomhnuill	Hinn, hainn hurra bhi!
Theich é leis an ropàn	Ni' Chaluim is Dhnomhnuill

In this next example, voice is recorded, sampled and blended with synthesiser sounds to produce a thick drone accompaniment. This activity is presented as a sample; similar activities could be planned from any songs built over a drone – the Marta Sebestyen, the Nusrat Fateh Ali Khan, and Bulgarian choir compact discs mentioned in the extended voice skills section (see pages 43-45), all contain tracks where vocal melodies are heard over vocal drones.

● ──

Sheila Chandra – *ABoneCroneDrone*

Each of the songs on the compact disc 'ABoneCroneDrone' by Sheila Chandra is founded upon a drone. The drone backings are created from recorded, layered voice sounds to which electronically produced sounds have been added. The studio techniques give a 'cosmic', mystical feel to the drone sound. Sheila Chandra is an Anglo-Asian singer who works cross-culturally taking the drone sounds characteristic of South Asian music and creating songs which mix styles drawn from pop, classical, folk songs, so-called world musics and 'new age' styles. She relies on studio techniques of layering, altering and adding to extend what she is able to produce as a solo singer.

Listen to track 3 and ask the children to listen for and hum the drone. Listen for the most dominant, lower sound first and then the less distinct higher sound. A little later a new pitch is heard against the drone and then disappears again followed by snatches of hummed vocal sounds, as if the drone and its harmonic notes turn like a mobile, catching the ear at different sound points. Rhythmic chanting on just two notes emerge from the drone as the piece develops. Short phrases of lyrical melody alternate with the chanting. These are sung to open vowel sounds in which Sheila Chandra uses the different timbres of her low and high voice registers.

Listening and joining in vocally is an effective way of engaging with this music, particularly to hum the drone and experience from inside the music how it holds on to and works with and against the chanting and melodic phrases. Similar background drone sounds could be created with a keyboard and added voice sounds recorded,

sequenced and blended. Recorded drone sounds could provide a
starting point for children's song composing.

---

repetitive patterns:

Drones can develop into simple repetitive patterns – ostinato
patterns – by moving onto new notes. Playing and experimenting
with moving drones, adding notes and variations is part of the
process of moving children towards independent part singing. This
is the focus of the activity which evolves from this next song, a folk
song from Israel.

Here are details for pronunciation of the words:
The comma after M' and hag' indicates a vowel sound, the
approximate vowel sound of 'good'.

Kol Do-dee hee-nay zay-bah
M' dah lay-gal hay-hah-reem
M' dah-pehts ahl hah-g' vah-ot ['o' as in Pole] (Goetze, 1984)

And in translation:
'The voice of my beloved; he is approaching, skipping upon the
mountains and dashing among the hills' (Goetze, 1984).

Once the children know the song well they can begin to hum drone notes which the melody suggests to secure their sense of the song's tonality – then begin to move away from the drone note and explore simple patterns to develop a second accompanying part. Here are some possibilities:

- sing the drone note as an anchor, then move from it to a new pitch and back again;
- the song itself can suggest melodic snatches which can develop into ostinati – the very first phrase, kol do-di, can be sung throughout and will create some wonderful musical relationships between the accompaniment and melody, particularly in the verse part;
- sing the drone-like patterns an octave higher above the melody – in an echo effect;
- combine more than one pattern in sequences or layers;
- plan for different accompaniments to the two parts of the song;
- work out a way to end the song (a coda) – the kol do-di pattern repeated and getting softer works well;
- plan the dynamics of melody and accompanying parts – e.g. are the dynamics of melody and accompaniment in balance? can interest be created by changing the dynamics of the accompanying parts?

The singing of simple ostinati parts which arise from the one, two, three chord harmonies of some songs and rounds will develop children's harmonic awareness of different chords and the movement from chord to chord. In this next song, a simple round, the harmony shifts from one chord to a new one and back again. First the children learn the melody of the round as a unison and only when it is securely known begin to explore the part-singing. The first bar, 'it is light', provides an ostinato which can be sung repetitively throughout and emphasises the harmonic change. Sing the round very slowly and softly, humming perhaps, in order to be able to dwell on the sounds of the two voice harmonies. Encourage the children to be aware of the other parts as they sing.

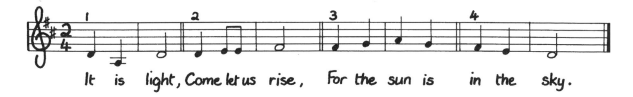

riffs

Just as in the distinction between drones and ostinati, the difference between an ostinato and a riff is hard to pin down. A riff is a term often used in pop and jazz to describe a repetitive bass pattern and, unlike an ostinato, a complete riff pattern will shift onto different pitches creating a more mobile harmonic effect. Riffs are often sung to the kind of 'shoo waddy waddy' syllables which children enjoy creating for themselves. It usually feels natural to move with the rhythm of the riff when singing – and again, once singing, the children can be encouraged to find their own simple swayings and step patterns.

The following riff:

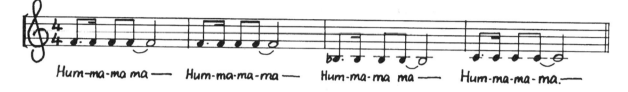

Hum-ma-ma ma — Hum-ma-ma-ma — Hum-ma-ma ma — Hum-ma-ma-ma.—

– provides a foundation for improvised melody singing above. Here is a melody that can be sung against it in a single line.

Ska - la - la - la — Ska - la - la - la — Ska - la - la - la — Ska - la - la.

| notice |

How children are managing all the different kinds of first part singing. Can they hold a single pitch drone note against a melody? can they maintain a simple ostinato part while others sing something different? can they find and hold a simple ostinato or riff that sounds out the lower notes of a small harmonic sequence?

two lines of melody together

When one melodic thread weaves in and out against one (or more) other threads of melody in counterpoint some of the most wonderful varieties of texture, of tension and release can be created. Round singing provides an accessible way in to first singing of independent vocal lines. A round is a circular song which is complete in itself if sung in unison but will double up with itself in two or more parts.

Sumer is icumen in 14th century round (rota). MS Harley 978. Reproduced by permission of the British Library.

rounds and canons

There seems little doubt that the round (or canon, catch, rota, roundel, to give some other names for rounds or songs of very similar type) is a particularly English form. The singing of rounds was a popular sociable pastime in homes, taverns and clubs and they were shared and passed on by ear long before the first collections were written down. Rounds and other short compositions in canon appear frequently in Renaissance anthologies of music – Henry VIII's manuscript contains examples of these including *Canon in Honour of Henry VIII* (British Library, Royal MS 11) (see page 167) and in the early seventeenth century Ravenscroft collected and published rounds along with partsongs and madrigals. This round was published in 1609 among Ravenscroft's first collection called 'Pammelia'.

Although this can be sung by as many as five singers, each entering at one bar intervals, it can be effectively sung by two singers following one another. The last bar is tricky but its rhythmic and melodic contrast to the other lines of the round is essential to the whole character of this old round. Collections of rounds intended for school use often edit this round into a simplified but less interesting form.

Popular in taverns and clubs, round-singing was essentially sociable and informal but largely, it would seem, the preserve of men – the very last of the 'gentlemen's catch clubs' in London was disbanded in 1915. Certainly the topics of many early rounds reflect a male perspective (Brewer, 1995) and many were blatantly bawdy. Eventually, in this century, round singing has become confined almost entirely to school and collectives of young people such as Scouts and Guides and the publications which are produced aim to satisfy this demand – albeit with adapted versions of the words and often simplified melodies for some old rounds to make them suitable for children. Round singing has persisted as a form of children's music for school use although its roots into the past share many of the same motivations for singing – sociability, an instant part singing effect which has an inviting immediacy, and the humorous, lighthearted nature of the words in the form of puns and plays on words are still part of many contemporary rounds written with children in mind. For teaching whole classes of children rounds have many advantages; once learnt in unison, they offer an instant way in to part-singing, the vocal range is fairly narrow which suits pre-adolescent voices and the different words 'fixing' each line helps the children to hold on to the independent melodies.

In England rounds are tied to a tradition of unaccompanied choral singing in communal settings. The compositional challenge of a round – to make a melody which will double back and harmonise with itself connects the composition of rounds with the skills of counterpoint writing. Collections of rounds and canons have been written by many composers writing notated music in the Western European classical tradition, Mozart, Schubert, Haydn to name but some. The musical puzzle of writing glorious melodies which gradually reveal the intricacies of their harmony as layer adds to layer appears to be the primary challenge. These are more complex rounds, written not for tavern rollicking but as well crafted miniatures.

Rounds have also found their way into collections of art songs written by composers in this century. Britten's collection 'Friday Afternoons' includes the round 'Old Abram Brown' for example and Nicola LeFanu's collection 'Rory's Rounds', intended for a primary school choir, is the source of this next round:

Rid-dle me ree, rid-dle me ree, A lit-tle man in a tree, A stick in his hand and a stone in his throat, If you tell me this rid-dle I'll give you a groat. ———(t)

In learning rounds it is important that the round is known securely in unison before moving into part-singing for the part singing magic will only be revealed if the singing is well in tune. When rehearsing rounds for performance there are many different formats for deciding how the part singing might work. These kinds of decisions are made by the singing group in the process of rehearsal. Here are some of the possibilities:

| to begin |
- all children sing the round in unison first and then move into singing in parts;
- one part begins and then the others follow turn by turn;

| to continue |
- when all the voices are singing their parts – decide how many times each voice will sing through the complete round;
- decide dynamics – sudden changes can be effective, or it might be appropriate to mark out harmonic changes by gradually getting louder or softer;

| to finish |
- voices drop out one by one leaving the last singer (or singers) to complete the melody alone;
- the singers can decide to end together, simultaneously. In some rounds the end of each line brings the singers to a final chord.

These are not hard and fast rules – but there are many variations in the way in which rounds can be sung. Groups of children – say, four children, two to a part, for a two-part canon – might work on a performance as a week's project. Not all the parts have to be sung – rounds sound effective with some instrumental and some vocal lines.

partsongs

There seems to be a gap between the part singing skills developed in simple drone and ostinati accompaniments, rounds and canons and the demands of holding a second vocal line which is quite independent of the first. Part of this difficulty may be purely pedagogical. If working with a whole class it can be quite difficult to manage the learning of two melodic lines by rote. Ideally children will learn both parts and be able to interchange the two. Part of the difficulty is also one of musical skills. The 'double listening' described earlier (see page 54) is an essential skill for pitching part against part and hearing one's own voice spaced harmonically from another voice. In contrast, much round singing can be relatively successful even with a low level of aural awareness for what other parts are doing. Aural awareness of and an imagination for part singing will be greatly supported by experience of listening to part singing across a wide range of styles. It is also very helpful if the children can frequently hear teachers and other adults singing a second part with their own voices.

activity

~ Returning once again to the first activities for improvising and experimenting with two part singing, the children improvise two separate melodic pathways, perhaps drawing them in the air with a finger or making pencil drawings on paper. These kinds of first activities will introduce many of the different ways in which two voices can join together.

Staggering and overlapping

Moving In the same direction, parallel

Coming together or diverging

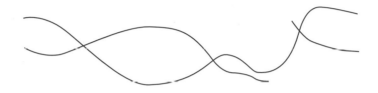

Improvising activities can provide preparatory activity for two songs. Studying song scores first will give many clues for how the two voices interact – staggered entries, echoing, movement in one part while the other moves little, movement in opposite directions and the final settling onto the same note. Listening to part music which demonstrates these techniques, for example the cantatas of Barbara Strozzi, helps singers to hear how two or more lines can relate.

●

singing in parallel parts: a fair wind's blowing

The next song was collected on a visit to Panama by Beatrice Landeck (1961) as part of her research into the folk songs of the Americas in the 1950s. She gives the song in translated form only, unfortunately without its original Spanish words. In this dance-song, as with many Latin-American songs, it sounds effective and in keeping with the song style to harmonise spontaneously in parallel thirds. Singing in parallel parts, thirds or other intervals can link with listening for and working with parallel parts and chordal harmonies on instruments, particularly barred instruments, xylophones, where the visual layout reinforces the aural awareness.

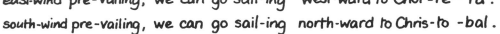

Getting started with the parallel part is usually the hardest point – in this song it can help the children to think of *'stepping up one note later to sing the lower part'* as shown in the notated sample which follows. A possible simple lower voice part for the solo section of the song is also suggested. This could be sung by the larger group to accompany the solo voice.

The Panamanian dance is called the 'tamborito' and is danced by one couple within a circle who sing, stamp feet and clap hands to accompany their dancing. The circle stamp on the beat and clap the off-beats (Landeck, 1961). For children to sing and simultaneously coordinate these movements is likely to require some practice and the tempo must be quite leisurely. Typically a group of instrumentalists might play for the dance on guitar, violin, drums of various sizes and maracas. The song can be accompanied throughout with the two chords of F and C – (or D and A chords if easier). Violinists can take the melody line and two rhythmic patterns in characteristic style are suggested for untuned percussionists.

individual progression

The development of children's singing skills was considered in the part on voice skills (see page 38). Listening experiences in school will aim to both recognise the children's out-of-school listening and to broaden and enrich it, making connections with a wide diversity of vocal music traditions. Children will already have a sure sense of style and know that solo artists develop their own distinctive performance style. At the same time children will continue the song making begun in the early years of primary school, developing both the improvised, spontaneous song-making and the worked out composition of songs using given song structures and word and melody ideas.

As they progress in the primary school children can learn vocal techniques which will equip them to use their voices in a range of different styles with some understanding of how to interpret and use their voices in performance. They will become assured as solo singers, perhaps following their own line of particular interest, and at the same time able to contribute their voices to group, ensemble or class choir singing. By the latter stages of primary school children will have learnt how to maintain a simple second part while a singer sings a complementary part. They will have listened to a wide range of vocal music and be able to discuss it with some understanding of simple song structures, vocal techniques and ways of setting words. They will also be able to analyse two part singing and apply a simple understanding of two voice part structures in talking about how the voices are interacting.

71

assessment points

early stages

The child:
- can control the pitch of their voice across a range appropriate for standard children's songs and knows some simple principles of voice technique;
- can join in simple voice games and improvised activities in which one voice sings independently to another;
- composes songs with some understanding of song forms.

later stages

The child:
- can control the voice appropriately in singing a repertoire of songs across a range of styles;
- can maintain a simple voice part with a partner who is singing a different melodic part;
- composes and performs songs showing creativity and a sensitivity to combinations of words and music.

primary music: later years

music for instruments

Music made with instruments opens up an entirely new set of possibilities, which run alongside those of music for voices, at times interweaving but often quite distinct. In world music terms, the instrumental music of a particular culture, whether folk or art music, frequently has its own separate roots, traditions and genres. These arise as a consequence both of the materials and technologies of the available instruments themselves and of the cultural practices associated with these alternatives to more immediately body-based music. In the art music traditions of Western Europe, instrumental music moved from association with dance forms and folk music, to incorporation into vocally-based domestic music in which instruments and voices might be used interchangeably, and on to independent instrumental forms such as those of chamber music, concertos and symphonies, whilst retaining an accompanying role for vocal music. Meanwhile, the instrumental forms of European traditional musics have remained fairly distinct from their vocal counterparts, yet popular music forms have mostly taken voice and instruments together.

For very young children, the music making worlds of voice and instruments are very distinct. The quite different physical demands of producing sound vocally or through extensions of the body actions of blowing, fingering, striking, scraping and so on, result in different kinds of improvised or composed musical patternings. Vocal and instrumental skill levels in performing, for example in recreating a melody, can also be far apart, with different hazards in each. The years between 7 and 11 see children move into a completely new phase of instrumental capability and this stage can be crucially important in the development of the skills of instrumental playing. This has major implications for both composing and performing activity. There is also a widening of outlook. During this phase, children are trying out and listening to different instruments, building on earlier acquired basic skills of controlling instrumental sound across a range of simple instruments, and making choices of particular instruments to learn to play long-term, perhaps even life-long. By the end of the age-phase most children have developed the physique, general motor skills and co-ordination needed for playing most instruments, so the potential for taking up lessons on one particular instrument widens as they move through the school. The general interest and motivation for skill acquisition across all kinds of activities, whether sporting, artistic or otherwise, which characterises this age-group, easily carries over into instrumental playing which is usually embarked on with enthusiasm.

This section looks first at some issues surrounding provision for instrumental learning within the mainstream music curriculum from 7–11. It outlines a framework for giving children a breadth of introductory experiences and the additional opportunity to focus on learning individual instruments in order to develop skills. This is particularly important because each instrument has its own often quite specialised skills, with relatively little scope for transferability from one to another. Practical ways of exploring music for instruments through composing, performing and listening are then suggested, starting with the possibilities of solo music and then music for two players. Finally, music making for small groups is considered. It is impossible to overestimate the importance of keeping music making closely linked to investigating and listening activities which open up the many and varied worlds of instrumental music. Learning to play or compose for an instrument entails having a lively understanding of how it can and might sound, just as the insights which come from first hand instrumental experience can be drawn on in listening and responding to live or recorded music. The process is reciprocal.

instrumental skills

Planning for instrument learning and skill development is unquestionably best done on a school-wide basis. There are so many different kinds of instruments and so many contexts for playing them, that varied groupings, including mixed-age groupings, can be a necessity if there is to be breadth of opportunity. If each child's instrumental learning is to progress and maintain continuity from term to term and year to year, the school must have an overall policy for the organisation of learning opportunities and for tracking all children's pathways through them. Whether instrumental work is being developed in class, in lunchtime or after school groups, or with visiting teachers, the class teacher has a vital co-ordinating role. Children will inevitably be following different programmes and it is for the class teacher to maintain an overview and make sure that everyone is provided for. The idea that 'sometimes using a bit of percussion' in the music lesson can cover any child's instrumental learning is a misconception which does justice neither to children nor to the instruments (nor to percussionists). Equally unhealthy is the situation in which a very small number of children having lessons on a 'real' instrument with a visiting teacher are treated as if this is a quite separate world or as if they are 'the musicians', set apart from everyone else. For each child, general and broad experience can be balanced by a sustained focus on acquiring skills on one or more instruments chosen from a whole spectrum of opportunities.

The foundations of successful practice in instrumental learning across the school lie in keeping a clear overview of how teaching will deal with some main issues.

- Planning must include all children. However instrumental teaching and learning is organised, there must be enough range of opportunity and enough differentiation to motivate and include everyone. The overall approach to offering opportunities, teaching, assessing and tracking progress must work within a consistent and common framework and be applied to every child.

- Planning should also be based on an inclusive view of the value of all instruments. Although there will always be resource limitations as to which instruments can be made available, the choice of instruments on offer should be as wide and open as possible in terms of musical style and ethnic origins. Hierarchies in which some instruments are considered more 'real', serious or valuable than others can be very limiting. A more positive outlook maintains a respect for the skills associated with playing any instrument and a valuing of the range of different kinds of music and playing styles reflected in a very diverse culture.

- Planning will need to make the best possible use of resources available, drawing on all available expertise and maximising use of teaching time. Provision can include opportunities for using instruments to accompany singing, playing instrumental music in small or large groups, including music composed by children, playing solo repertoire and improvisation.

What does this mean in practice? The framework suggested here aims to balance general, class-based provision which introduces a broad range of instruments and music with opportunities for learning specific instruments in a more sustained way so that progress can be made in building skills and understanding.

introducing instruments

Moving on from their early years work, children should have gathered a fair amount of basic hands-on experience with instruments across the range of categories. The following classification (Hornböstel in Sachs, 1940) is a useful basis for introducing different sorts of instruments to children, both in relation to listening and to ensure that they gain some early playing experience across the full range.

- aerophones: *wind instruments, where sound is produced by the vibration of air; e.g. pipes, flutes, reeds, whistles, ocarinas, brass, mouth organs;*
- chordophones: *stringed instruments, where sound is produced by the vibration of strings; e.g. fiddle, harp, zither, guitar, viols and violins, bows, and strung keyboards;*
- idiophones: *made of material that is naturally sonorous without being stretched or altered; e.g. rattles, jingles, claves, bells, gongs, xylophones, metallophones, scrapers, mbira;*
- membranophones: *where the sound is produced by the vibration of a stretched skin; e.g. drums of every kind, kazoos;*
- electrophones: *where the sound is produced by means of an electrical current: guitars, keyboards, synthesisers; electric fiddles.*

(More details of choice, provision and early activities with instruments are given in *Music in the Early Years*, (Young and Glover, 1998).)

Children will have experienced making music with instruments of different kinds which are blown, plucked, struck, shaken, scraped. They will have learnt how to vary timbre, duration, pitch and dynamics on different instruments and to associate larger sizes of instrument with generally lower pitches, and so on. It is well worth checking at the beginning of this age-phase for gaps in this experience, particularly in relation to the range of instruments. It may be the case that almost all instruments encountered have been, for example, percussion instruments, in which case a focus will be needed on instruments which are blown or plucked. Where this broad early experience is lacking, whatever the age of the children, it will need to be provided; this forms an essential basis of understanding for use of instruments in composing or accompanying, for listening and investigating music, and for making choices about instruments to be learnt in a longer term way.

A breadth of exploratory work across the range of instruments also needs to be sustained for all children through the later primary years in order to extend and build on this wider understanding. A good quality range of instruments covering the above categories is essential for general use and a system for storage, easy access and availability across all classes can be arrived at, understood and used by everybody. Introductory work gives children opportunities to use a full range of instruments for music making (see later) and to find out more about their uses and musical characteristics. It needs to be challenging, detailed and at as high a level as is appropriate to the level of understanding of the children, and can best be planned for within the scope of each class's music and in a way which integrates different kinds of musical activity. For example:

| activity | ~ Two or three children are asked to do some initial research on South American percussion instruments with reference to CDs and books or CD-ROM on world musical instruments; they make a presentation to the class of their findings, passing round pictures and including musical sound if possible. The class as a whole take part in a sorting exercise with the school's percussion instrument collection, sorting out instruments a) which are of South American origin and b) which are used in South American music. This is followed by listening to instrumental music from one or more South American countries, by practical exploration of dance rhythms associated with e.g. samba and by rehearsal by a small group of children of a song or dance, using appropriate instruments. |

As children move through the age-range, interest is sustained by supplementing class work with workshops or performances by visitors, introducing particular instruments or types of music. High priority can be given to instruments which are represented at classroom level e.g. percussion, keyboards, guitar. If these inputs are well balanced across a wide range of musical interests they can be an invaluable additional stimulus for instrumental work. Visitors might be older children, students in sixth form or college and local amateurs as well as professional performing groups.

Opportunities can be provided for simple activities which allow children to use instruments as they discover more about them. Even if carried out in a whole class setting, it is usually better if only a few instruments are in use at any one time since quality of listening is paramount.

activities

~ Work out simple accompaniments to whole class or small group singing, using one or two carefully chosen instruments. Think about exactly what timbre is wanted, and what the instruments will play: a rhythm pattern which repeats or changes, a drone, one line of a round repeated, a sequence of one or two chords. Try out, listen and modify.

~ Make instrumental improvisations for 3 or 4 players using a basic structure such as 'take turns to play', 'join in one at a time', 'add a different pattern', 'copy and change'. Use a listening group who can also suggest new 'rules' to be tried out. Think about the character of the role each instrument takes and how it complements or contrasts with others.

learning an instrument

Assuming that provision is made for ongoing introductory instrumental experience, attention also needs to be given to the pathway each child will follow in building instrumental skills of their own. If children are to acquire instrumental experience and skills progressively as they move through the 7–11 age-phase, then each child needs some opportunity to *stay with* one particular instrument for long enough to acquire technical skills and to practise and use these in musical contexts. This aspect of instrumental learning has sometimes been left entirely to chance, with the result that many children miss out altogether. It is in providing for continuity of instrumental experience, whether throughout a year or through this age-phase and beyond, that whole-school planning for flexible provision is most needed. There is a need here for wide differentiation and for a willingness to allow for:

● different musical styles and contexts;
● different levels of learning;
● different mixtures of large and small group learning;
● mixed age teaching;
● different time spans for opting in; time out where appropriate;
● opportunities for changes of instrument;
● links to extra provision outside the school.

This approach entails every child choosing to concentrate on one particular instrument, long or shorter term, but with a clear purpose of building skills and understanding. Here individual preference becomes a key issue since instruments differ enormously. They differ in:

● their timbre: *the quality of sound*;
● how they are played: *blown, bowed, beaten*;
● the kind(s) of music they are associated with: *folk, classical, pop, jazz etc. and across different times and places*;
● the musical role they take: *melodic, harmonic, bass line, rhythmic*;
● the size, shape, pitch range, and character they have.

Instruments are simply not interchangeable. Children will often have strong views about which instruments they would like to learn and it pays dividends to listen to these preferences and take them seriously where possible. Being successful in playing an instrument, sustaining progress, feeling good and sounding musical are intrinsically bound up with its being the right instrument for the right person. And rightness is strongly linked to personality, self-image and taste in relation to the differences above, as well as to having an appropriate physical build (Ben-Tovim, 1979).

Gender stereotyping has also been shown to operate strongly in relation to instrumental choice. Certain instruments are generally perceived as being more masculine, e.g. brass instruments, or feminine, e.g. the flute. Bruce and Kemp (1993) demonstrate that even very young children's instrumental preferences are influenced by observations of the sex of players in visiting instrumental groups. O'Neill (1997) showed that older children can be subject to bullying related to learning instruments which cross perceived gender boundaries. In order to maintain open opportunities for children to choose to learn instruments which run counter to stereotypical norms, schools have to be alert to monitoring in order to maintain the balance of models represented among the staff, in visiting groups and on audio and video tape or CD.

Lateral thinking is needed about the range of instruments (as well as voice) used for more sustained individual learning. These might include:

- wind instruments: e.g. tin whistle, ocarina, recorder, panpipe, transverse pipes/fife, bagpipes, flute, single reed e.g. clarinet, saxophone, or double e.g. oboe, bassoon;
- plucked string instruments: e.g. guitar – folk, classical, or electric (lead or bass), mandolin, sitar, zither, harp;
- bowed string instruments: violin, viola, 'cello, double bass; early instruments e.g. rebec, fiddle, viols;
- keyboard instruments: electric keyboards, piano, harmonium, accordion;
- percussion: kit drums, snare drum, tabla, timpani, African drums, conga, steel band, small percussion, xylophone (chromatic), glockenspiel (chromatic), hand-bells, suspended bells (tubular, medieval);
- brass: bugle, cornet, trumpet, tenor horn, french horn, trombone, baritone, euphonium, tuba.

These instruments range from very cheap to almost prohibitively expensive; availability of the latter depends on school or county provision or on children using instruments the family already have or buy. Each school has to make decisions about which instruments to invest in and how to plan their use. Decisions are often best made in conjunction with planning for a range of different performing groups. For example, a school may choose to set up a steel band, an early music group including recorders, percussion and strings, and a brass ensemble and to buy and maintain instruments relevant to these. Other groups may be run as available activities for large groups of children but depend on parents supplying the instruments, for example, guitars or penny whistles. Others again might run by a mixture of parent and school investment and by advertising and collecting locally e.g. keyboards or accordions. Finally, the school may provide access to specialist teachers but leave funding to parents, both in paying for lessons and hiring or buying instruments. This is how lessons on orchestral instruments are often managed. Some children may be receiving tuition at home e.g. on piano, or through membership of youth groups e.g. brass bands, marching bands, boys brigade, etc. These children are learning skills which can be used and extended in groups at school.

Instrumental learning needs to be negotiated with each child and then tracked. The class teacher makes sure that each child is involved in some ongoing way with a strand of individual instrumental playing and learning. This might be through intermittent membership of groups which meet for a limited period e.g. half a term or a more permanent commitment. Or it might be through an individual 'contract' to focus on a particular instrument in class lessons with additional time to practise alone. Once a school wide system is established, with parents and children involved, this can run very simply. Time spent in the initial organisation is more than compensated for by the increased motivation which results. The vital components of tracking each child are:

- make sure that the child has a clear plan for instrumental work for the term or year and that this is agreed between child, class teacher and any other teacher(s) involved;
- make sure each child logs their plans in their music notebooks, including some specific learning aims agreed with individual or group instrumental teachers;
- make sure it's clear to everyone when work will happen e.g. whether it is weekly throughout the year or for six weeks after Christmas leading up to a concert and then again in the summer term;

As work progresses:
- help children plan practice times and routines, in school or at home as appropriate; include use of listening helpers to encourage in-school practice;
- make sure each child makes use of their instrumental skills in class activities;

- encourage each child to make notebook entries tracking their own progress against agreed learning aims and also to make entries recording and reflecting on music played and listened to, including particular performers heard;
- make sure each child and each relevant teacher contributes to assessment and record keeping at agreed points e.g. twice yearly;
- make sure that each child can describe their own progress, level of learning and range of instrumental experience; this is a key part of ensuring good continuity as the child moves on to a new class or school.

performing with instruments

As children move through this age-phase, it becomes harder to generalise about performing experience. It is clearly important that the work done in acquiring instrumental skills is given meaning through plenty of different opportunities for playing, alone and with others. Some of this will be organised through instrumental teachers and through groups in which children are learning. This can be balanced by opportunities which allow individual children to play in different groupings, to a range of audiences, formal and informal, and to become used to adapting their skills to different music making situations. Class teachers have a vital role in keeping an overview, making sure that each child has a range of opportunities and that instrumental groups mix and match as far as possible.

It is useful if there is a common set of learning aims for instrumental performance which is agreed and worked to by all teachers who contribute, whatever the instrument or group in question. This can include a range of experiences to be built, together with learning looked for. For example:

- learning solo pieces and performing them to others in the group; *learning the music itself, learning how to practise; experimenting and making decisions about interpretation e.g. tempo, dynamics; presenting music confidently to a group of listeners;*
- accompanying a song sung by a group or class; *working out an accompanying part e.g. doubling the tune, playing choruses only, playing a different melody, giving a rhythm or chordal backing etc; learning the part with singers or alone; learning how to fit in*

with singers and follow;

● playing duets with same and different instruments; *learning to play an independent part; collaborating in rehearsing together; starting and stopping at the same time; working expressively with someone else – listening and communicating; understanding the needs of other instruments e.g. to breathe, change beaters.*

These objectives can be applied across the whole range, including 'classroom' instruments, percussion, and all instruments learned in groups or individually.

exploring instrumental music

The following series of practical investigations aims to help children to discover and understand the characteristics and potential of individual instruments and to explore the different textures which can be created in music for one, two or more players. Every instrument has its own characteristic solo repertoire, reflecting its origins, construction and capabilities. Music for two players introduces the dimension of musical interaction and the textures and structures that derive from this. Music for three, four or five players includes, in world music terms, most music for small ensemble; in terms of children working in the classroom, five is probably a realistic top limit for most small groups working together.

These investigations are approached particularly through composing; ideas for this are gathered by listening to a wide range of music. The activities also lend themselves to being closely linked with children's individual instrumental learning, as another source of finding out more about the qualities and range of particular instruments and the playing techniques that belong to them. This work can be made as challenging as children can manage and offers lots of scope for extension for able and musically experienced children. At its simplest, however, it is accessible to everybody and can be used to develop understanding of musical structures and composition techniques. The musical ideas here can cross stylistic boundaries without difficulty and can be adapted to work for instrumentalists in any genre.

planning points

These activities can be introduced in small stages over a long time-scale. An approach of 'visiting' this strand from time to time, alongside the wider development of instrumental performing skills is ideal. As ever, the actual materials and ideas are indicative only and will work best when adapted to match particular children's musical needs and interests. Ideas can be introduced and explored through whole class work but the best composing will be done by individuals having the opportunity to work alone or with a small group of players who make input as performers but not as composers. Such opportunities inevitably have to be spread out over time on a rolling programme. The music which results can be incorporated into class repertoire, played at informal listening sessions or class or school concerts; this endorses the valuing of children's work and encourages children to move confidently between performing and composing.

The help of visiting performers, instrumental teachers, and others who play instruments, whether parents, friends or pupils from nearby secondary schools or colleges, is invaluable. The school may also need a policy of building resources, adding gradually to the collection of recordings until there is at least one example of a solo piece for every instrument learnt or heard live in the school and a wide range of music for small groups of players.

music for one

The idea of music for just a single instrument may seem at odds with much of the music we hear most immediately around us, particularly if the instrument is, or is predominantly, also a single-line instrument such as a flute or saxophone. A great deal of the music with which children are familiar is for smaller or larger performing groups. So a good way to start investigating music for one player is to ask children to start listening out for examples wherever they are, and to bring their findings into school, either by describing what they've heard or if possible bringing recordings or live players. This relates well to pupils' own learning situation; they will also be able to play and record examples of music they are learning themselves on particular instruments and talk about these.

In fact, of course, music for one is a huge category of instrumental music. This music is widely represented in folk traditions world-wide, particularly for instruments such as pipes and flutes, fiddles, guitars, or reed instruments. There is also a large repertoire of art music for unaccompanied solo instruments, for instance, Bach's six 'sonatas for violin alone' and six 'suites for 'cello alone'. More contemporarily, Luciano Berio's series of *Sequenzas*, each written for a different instrument, for a particular performer, explore virtuosity and extended techniques of producing sound in ways which stretch both instrument and player to their limits.

Investigating music for single instruments of any of the above kinds has several advantages for developing composers. It is a good way for children to continue to build a detailed and thorough understanding of the sounds and possibilities of specific instruments. This work takes pupils far beyond simply recognising and naming instruments heard. They begin to build the kind of specific knowledge a composer needs in order to write well for a chosen instrument, rather than just writing a tune which could be played on more or less anything. It allows them to:

- increase their aural awareness of all the different ways one instrument can sound;
- concentrate on exploiting the particular potential of the instrument chosen;
- deepen their working knowledge of the range of timbre, of pitch, of playing techniques and of what is practical or not, easy or difficult to play;
- compose for themselves or others as performers, working within appropriate skill levels;
- build up comparative knowledge of the different requirements when composing for different instruments.

Music for one instrument is an aspect of composing which can be revisited many times as children gradually widen their knowledge of different instruments and of musical possibilities. It should build progressively throughout this age range and on into the next. As composers, given this grounding, children are gradually able to identify their own preferences for the sound and character of certain instruments over others and to extend their imaginative use of instrumental choice.

investigating individual instruments

Music composed for one instrument playing alone can be thought of in three main categories:

- music for pitched instruments which basically produce only one note at a time resulting in a single musical line;
- music for pitched instruments which also have harmonic possibilities, such as accordion, guitar, marimba, mbira, lute or piano;
- music for solo unpitched percussion, for example all kinds of drums and double drums.

(Music for bagpipes and hurdy-gurdies could be added to either of the first two groups, since these are basically single-line instruments but with harmonic drones built in.)

Children can be encouraged to work across all three categories at different times; they each pose different challenges.

The following activities lay the groundwork for building understanding as a listener and the basic knowledge needed for any instrumental composing. They should be returned to as an initial research stage whenever a new instrument is encountered.

activities

~ Carry out an investigation of one instrument. Work alone or in a pair and bring the results to the class session. Be ready to talk about and demonstrate the range of instrumental sounds and effects; listen to the *range* of sounds available across each musical element. For example, investigate:
  - timbre – what variations in sound quality can be made a) by the usual techniques of playing the instrument b) by extending these techniques e.g. playing the violin strings with the wooden side of the bow, moving fingers on flute keys without blowing; playing the xylophone with finger tips;
  - pitch – how far apart are the highest and lowest sounds available? make a class chart comparing the ranges of different instruments for reference when composing; add to it gradually as new instruments are investigated; use letter names, count

notes and represent on a bar chart, show fingerings or use standard notation if some children can read this;

- duration – what are the longest and shortest available sounds? how do you sustain or damp (stop) sounds?
- dynamics – what are the loudest and quietest sounds available? how do you gradually get louder or quieter ? what ways are there of accenting sounds?

How much does all this depend on the player's skills?

What kind of sounds are difficult to manage on this instrument? Why?

Which patterns of notes (if a pitched instrument) are easiest or hardest to play? Why?

For example, reasons might be: fingering patterns make it hard; crossing strings makes it hard; managing the two sticks or mallets makes it hard.

- Listen carefully to a recording of the chosen instrument being played, either completely alone or in the foreground of a group piece. Describe to a partner or the class what you notice about:
  - the sound of the instrument;
  - the kind of music the composer has given it to play;
  - how the performer plays the music.

Describe your own reactions to the sound and the music.

Examples can be chosen to give a range of perspectives. Listening to a violin playing a traditional Yiddish melody, a Scottish reel, a lyrical Edwardian parlour favourite such as Elgar's *Chanson de Matin*, or a Vivaldi concerto will each give another dimension to its capabilities. The following example shows the kind of discoveries that might be made. This particular choice opens children's ears to the possibilities of an instrument related to the classroom xylophone and shows the imaginative scope available.

Keiko Abe – *Michi*

Michi by Keiko Abe for marimba (a deep version of an orchestral xylophone, also a folk instrument) is recorded by Evelyn Glennie as an improvised piece which starts with single repeated notes reverberating and building towards patterns of two, three and more notes. As the music develops the listener hears many different ways of using mallets, combining the two 'hands', and patterning across a keyed instrument to give an effect of layers. The composer is also a marimba virtuoso; she has been determined to establish the instrument as a solo instrument and includes Japanese folk music, popular and classical music in her repertoire.

Alternatively,

↝ As a class or individually, make a list of some questions you think any composer will need answers to in order to compose music for a particular instrument. For example:

- which notes can be played on the instrument?
- how much breath is needed to hold a note on?
- what can't the instrument do? what can it do best?

Listen to a friend or visiting performer play. Does hearing the music answer any of your questions? Put any unanswered questions to the players.

↝ Think about the character the instrument has for you. Does it suggest a particular kind of music or any musical ideas which just seem to match? It might help to think of the instrument just like a character with a voice. What kind of music might this voice make? The music might follow expected ideas or experiment with unexpected ones.

Listening to particular instruments will suggest quite clearly different musical possibilities. These can be tried out by imitative improvising on a similar or different instrument. For example:

- music played on the shakuhachi, the Japanese end-blown flute, might suggest ideas of making melodic shapes with a single line, of varying the intensity of sound (in this case by techniques of blowing), of using a wide dynamic range, of using slow and sustained sound incorporating held notes and silences; *a recorder player, a clarinettist and a violinist might each try some of these ideas on their own instruments;*
- a section of a Bach solo 'cello partita might introduce the idea of structures built of patterns, of strongly rhythmic or lyrical dance music, of creating the illusion of more than one instrument at times, or of music that's hard to play: *a 'cellist, a keyboard and a xylophone player might each try some music using similar kinds of patterning;*

composing for one instrument

With the preliminary work in mind, children can compose a solo instrumental piece for themselves or someone else to play. It is better to keep the brief simple i.e. *'make a piece for xylophone'* than to introduce all kinds of other constraints with the intention of giving more structure. If good investigative work has been done, lots of ideas for music will already be flowing from what the instrument shows of itself. This is the best place of all from which to launch a piece and the best source of structures which arise from the instrument's own capabilities.

Here are some possibilities for ways into composing a piece for one instrument. Children can be encouraged to take whichever is most appropriate.

↝ *Decide on an overall idea for the piece*
Design a plan for how the piece might be as a whole. Examples might be:
- a piece that uses the lovely rich sound low down on the clarinet, uses it for a smooth tune;
- a piece which is rhythmic and bouncy because that's how the xylophone sounds if you play it quite fast;
- a piece for tambourine which has lots of loud and some very quiet bits and you don't know what's coming next;
- a piece for guitar which uses slides as well as plucked and strummed sounds, making a mysterious atmosphere.

Then compose music to match the plan by playing or by showing the player what you want.

↝ *Improvising first, composing later*
The player improvises, ideally recording the music for listening to again. The improvisation might be quite freely making it up or perhaps concentrating on one aspect of the discoveries above, for example, on the possibilities of the violin played pizzicato. Gradually the composer (who may or may not be the player) chooses how the music might go and goes on listening and making decisions until the piece is 'fixed'.

↝ *Sound patches*
Compose some 'sound patches' which you think sound particularly good on this instrument. These are short bits of ideas, rather like a

colour sample or a stitch sample, detailed but not joined up in the context of a whole piece. Again they can be based on investigations carried out. Collect lots of these in your notebook or on tape. Choose one or more and turn them into a piece or just save them in case they come in useful for a piece another time.

~ *Beginning ideas*
Compose a beginning idea – a single note, a bit of melody, an effect. Concentrate on what the chosen instrument can do best and imagine the effect of silence being broken with this idea. Go on to think of ways to play around with the beginning and develop it or, alternatively, what to follow it with. You may need to compose several beginnings in order to find one which can be developed in this way.

musical structures for one

As children become more experienced, they can begin to consider different ways in which composers structure music for one instrument. For example:
- a simple one line melody such as a dance tune, or a lament;
- a piece which explores timbre and the drama of dynamics and silence;
- a piece based on rhythmic patterning;
- a free improvisatory melodic piece e.g. Debussy – *Syrinx;*
- a piece structured in a classical form e.g. a dance form or two or three section form.

Some children may be ready to try one of these for themselves. Listening to examples or looking carefully at pieces they've learned to play already will always help.

listening skills

Practise the process of *'hear it, think it, hear it;'* this can be done with short fragments of music for any single instrument in order to build up the ability to imagine specific instrumental sound, to hear it in your head.

Sketch or colour on paper to show timbre – quality of sound – of music heard. Patches of vivid timbres are played on different instruments or, better still, patches of different timbre on the same instrument. Children record the quality of the sound by drawing each.

Use voices to match instrumental timbres, either through singing a melody e.g. with a tone like a flute, or just echoing instrumental effects. Match must be very accurate, not roughly similar.
Listen to an instrument playing. Collect vocabulary to describe the sound of the music.

focus on

- experiencing a wide range of rich and different timbres; being able to imagine the sounds precisely;
- knowing which playing techniques cause each sound;
- being able to use vocabulary to describe sound qualities heard or imagined.

music for two

Composing for any number of instruments will always involve the same preliminary investigations of the instruments themselves and what they can do. The following activities assume that this initial preparation has been done. They focus on the musical structures that can be used when making music for two instruments together.

interacting musically

A useful way for children to begin to understand the musical possibilities of structures for two instruments is to practise improvisations with a partner. If, in the early years, children have experienced music-making in twos – sharing an instrument and taking turns with an adult perhaps, or joining in with another child, keeping together or finding patterns that fit – they will be ready to begin to think about different ways in which music can be composed for two players. However much or little experience they have, they will benefit from ongoing opportunities to improvise with another player. This might take the form of:

- just making it up as you go along, seeing what happens, noticing 'good bits';

- having a 'conversation' and sometimes both 'talking at once';
- deciding on a 'rule' and then following it, e.g. only using certain notes, or always going on from where the other player leaves off.

Sometimes it will be useful to tape record the music and listen to it afterwards. Or two can improvise while another group, or the class, listens. As they listen, children notice, remember and then describe to the players what they hear. For example, the audience may notice the two players keeping in time but playing different things, or copying, or one instrument accompanying the other in a background role. Two children facing each other and working with a xylophone and a glockenspiel found that 'copying', that is, copying the playing action, came out sounding 'opposite'; in other words, it was an inversion – one tune went up and the other came down. They improvised for a while finding different mixtures of copying the sound and turning patterns upside down and backwards. They tried playing at the same time as well as one after another. This turned into a piece composed for these two instruments. Many such possibilities are more elaborately worked out in Britten's *Gemini Variations*, written for two players using several different instruments.

Musical interactions reflect social interactions and musical structures often grow out of these. Improvised music may start to take a shape from a 'leader and follower' structure, or a partnership in which one says little and one says a lot, from working harmoniously together, or having an energetic altercation. Improvisation might also focus on a particular element e.g. dynamics, duration, or timbre. Interactions can explore combinations of matching, continuing, contrasting or complementing. Players can listen to the effects of mixing or blending particular effects e.g. one recorder playing long notes, moving very slowly, while another plays a faster moving line against it. Two players on one keyboard can try contrasts of a smooth, joined-up line with very short, detached notes. Improvising is a good way to discover how the timbres of two different instruments sound when they play at different pitches or how the volume of the two balances up.

music for two

Alongside taking part in improvisations, children need to hear music for two players and to think about both the composing and the performing aspects of the music. Best of all is to invite children, visiting instrumental teachers or other performers to visit and play one or two duets for the class to hear. Limiting the programme to just a few examples will give an opportunity for discussion and investigation along the following lines:

- what roles do the two instruments have in the music? are they the same, different, equal? how? how is the music built?
- what has the composer given each instrument to do? what timbres and playing techniques are used?
- what is the overall effect of the piece on the listener?
- what skills do you need to play this piece together?

Steve Reich – *Clapping Music for Two Performers*

For example, in Steve Reich's *Clapping Music for Two Performers*, one performer keeps to the same pattern all the way through. The other has a pattern based on the first, but it shifts along in sections so that each time there is a different relationship between the two. The effect of the piece is mesmerising as the listener tries to follow the very small changes. The piece is very hard to play; it needs the skills of keeping rhythm very steady and of listening to the other player without being put off by them.

Reich writes, 'I composed clapping music out of a desire to create a piece of music that would need no instruments at all beyond the human body… In *Clapping Music* it can be difficult to hear that the second performer is in fact always playing the same original pattern as the first performer, though starting in different places'.

A similar approach can be taken to hearing recorded music for two players or seeing a performance on video. The same questions can be considered and the class can try to imagine how the composer was thinking and the experiences of the performers.

composing music for two

➳ In pairs or as a class, gather ideas from improvising and listening for ways in which music for two players might be constructed. The list might go something like this:

- they play the same instrument and the same music, keeping together;
- each player has their own tune but the tunes fit together;
- one player keeps a steady beat and the other plays music over it;
- there are two or three musical ideas which both players share, playing together and at different times;
- one player has a tune and the other plays chords which accompany it;
- the music is like a drama between two people; first they argue and then they manage to agree;
- two players share the same instrument; one plays higher and one lower;
- they play in a round, the same tune but one following the other;
- they alternate with each other, answering, copying, or contrasting, standing a little way apart.

➳ Choose one of these descriptions as a plan and compose a piece of your own for two players. The music will need to be composed using instruments or a computer so that the composer can hear what the music sounds like; it is also useful to record the music in draft stages and when it is finished.

Joint compositions, made by two children can work well if the children have reasonably compatible ideas. It is important though that each child sometimes has the opportunity to take all the decisions, to compose single-handedly. This is easy to manage by agreeing at the outset that, for instance, *'this is "Cassie's piece" which Cassie and Maeve are playing together'*.

As soon as children start working with two pitched instruments together, the dimension of harmony comes into the picture. To begin with, a good basis is for the composer simply to listen and decide what they like the sound of. Pitch is not necessarily the foreground element in younger children's listening and there may not be any issue about whether one player's 'tune' fits with the other's, from the children's point of view. When it does become an issue, children can be introduced to different note sets and the idea of composing music using a chosen scale, mode, or key. It is still important to encourage listening and decisions based on the sound as the best basis. It is a strength to be able to work with different note sets and this will be reflected in the music they hear if it is broad ranging in style.

listening skills

Listen to music for two players. Practise listening to the music as a whole and also listening to follow each part separately. Is it possible to do both at the same time?

When playing music with someone else, try to listen to what they are doing and hear how your part fits with it. This can be practised in a simpler way by just matching a simple beat on one note or a repeating pattern, keeping together, perhaps changing the balance from foreground to background.

Listen for the musical processes of copying, echoing, changing, fitting, following, developing. It may be possible to sketch an outline of how this happens in part or all of a simple piece.

Listen for the 'drama' of how the two instruments interact with each other in the music.

focus on

- hearing both parts together and the musical effects this gives;
- noticing the different ways in which music for two instruments can be constructed;
- comparing the techniques used in different pieces of music for two.

music for groups

Once the number of musical parts reaches beyond two, following each part as a listener becomes much more challenging. Often we hear the music as a whole and wouldn't necessarily pick out the separate lines which are contributing, nor be able to say how they are doing so.

An investigation of exactly how music for three or more players is put together can open up a whole range of musical formats. And some idea of how these might work is extremely useful if children are to compose their own music using a greater number of singers/players.

Once again, a first stage is to collect examples of music for say, three, four or five musicians and start to listen to and look at what each player in the group is actually doing. There is an enormous range of repertoire, particularly when music of different times and places is considered in addition to popular, folk, jazz and classical styles. Once children start to investigate by listening, it becomes clear that there is also an endless number of different ways of using a group of players. Certain musics are based on particular formats. For example, in the very complex tradition of North Indian classical music, a standard format would be that of a principal solo instrumentalist, perhaps on a sitar or sarangi, taking the lead, improvising within understood conventions and practice, a second player accompanying with a sustained drone played on tambura and a third playing tabla – pitched rhythmic drumming which interacts very skilfully with the main pitched instrument. A jazz ensemble will often incorporate a section of perhaps keyboard, bass and percussion with the function of keeping the harmony and rhythm going while other instruments work over this in a more elaborate and improvisatory way. This is not unlike a Baroque trio sonata in which a continuo of keyboard and cello, viewed as having one role and notated as such, lay down the harmonic foundation for the two solo instruments to play over. Other jazz formations may pass improvisatory or foreground roles more evenly round the group, each player in turn taking a spotlight.

The following sections each introduce one starting point for listening, composing and performing based on small group formats. Each is suggested by a different kind of music and the possibilities for inventing more are limitless. A key in this work is to allow listening to music in itself to suggest ideas for the children to investigate further. While knowledge anyone has already is useful, it is not a pre-requisite. Composition work in particular is always best if it is based on thoughtful listening and questioning, rather than on pre-planned recipes.

percussion groups

Music for a small percussion group can be an interesting way into investigating how three or more players can be used in an ensemble. Exploration through composition linked to listening can be the starting point. Children can work with unpitched instruments and focus on finding different mixtures and blends of timbre and texture from the extraordinary range of sonorities these instruments offer. Pitched and unpitched instruments can be combined, perhaps using instruments of one particular material. Listening to a percussion ensemble such as *Les Percussions de Strasbourg* will help to stimulate ideas for how such instruments can be used. In the following example the pieces are for percussion which can be related to instruments found in school and it is good for children to hear these instruments played professionally and brilliantly.

Xenakis – *Pleiades*

Xenakis's *Pleiades* is a set of four pieces, of which even the titles suggest some interesting ways of selecting instruments:

1 Melanges	(mixing, blending)	
2 Metaux	(metals – chimes, bells, tubular bells…)	
3 Claviers	(keyed instruments including keyboards, vibraphones, xylophones)	
4 Peaux	(skins – drums of all sorts)	

Xenakis's compositions are complex, but this doesn't detract from the richness of sound colour; children can learn a great deal from the imaginative palette alone. The music combines different rhythmic layers, repetitions and transformations so that the relationship of one part to another is extremely difficult for a listener to analyse, though the effects are none the less striking. The Pleiades are a constellation of seven stars, virgin sisters in Greek mythology. The music is described as 'sweeping the listener up into its whirlwind …… as if towards an inevitable catastrophe or towards a contorted universe'.

activity

The idea of these four pieces can be adapted as the basis for group pieces which explore combinations of timbre and texture.

~ Make a piece for three or four players using one of Xenakis's
   categories of sound.
~ Make a score of the outline framework of the music.

This music may particularly lend itself to the use of a semi-graphic score,
a map of the instruments' timbres, starting and stopping, and the
textures that result. Specific rhythms can be indicated where possible. For
more precision, the score can be drawn in five second blocks.

<table>
<tr><td>focus on</td><td>● imaginative use of percussive sound, sense of timbre and colour;
● ability to listen to and work with texture and layers, rhythmic or melodic.</td></tr>
</table>

using technology

Keyboards and drum machines with memory, computer composing
software, and multi-track recording equipment all offer a model for
composing music for several instruments which is based on the
process of layering. Working with these introduces children to
another way of thinking about music in several parts. The
underlying process is of playing, entering or recording a single line
of music, produced by a particular sound or voice, and saving this.
It can then be played back and another line composed to fit with it.
This can be entered in real time, that is, played in at the speed the
music will be heard, or in 'step time' bit by bit in the composer's
own time. Additional layers can be added according to the
composer's choice and the capacity of the technology. The music
can be saved and heard as electronic music; alternatively, the
technology can be used as a composing tool only, and the music
transferred onto acoustic instruments and performed by a group of
players.
The benefits of this are that it by-passes some of the difficulties of
performing and of trying to work with different parts when it is too
hard to imagine in the mind what the music will sound like. A child
can work as a solo composer and construct music for several parts.
The process can involve listening and altering; on a computer it can
include using editing tools like 'copy', 'cut' and 'paste' as for word-
processing. The linear approach, of devising one line, then adding
another and another, can be seen as both a strength and a possible
drawback. Composing a single line at a time ensures that the
'horizontal' aspect of the music works well; adding lines one at a

time is not always a very good way to construct the 'vertical' or harmonic dimension of the music.

- working processes which arise from using technology as a compositional tool e.g. sequencing and layering;
- the interaction between technology skills and listening skills;
- musical use of the extended opportunities offered by technology.

traditional bands

Listening to a range of examples of small groups playing music for dance or entertainment leads well into children arranging and performing music in similar formats themselves. Instrumental combinations vary and the roles of each instrument in a line-up can be considered. Very often, for instance, there is a melody instrument, a harmony instrument and percussion. *Music of the Andes* by the group Caliche, includes many examples of this and similar arrangements using panpipes or flute, guitar or similar strummed instrument and drum. A Morris dance side is often accompanied by a fiddle and accordion, with the dancers' bells, sticks and feet supplying the percussive element.

According to children's instrumental abilities, similar performing groups can be established to play their own or traditional music. At simplest this can be a drummer keeping a beat, a single chord played on guitar or keyboard (using single finger chord play), and a tune improvised over on any pitched instrument. Children with more advanced skills can find tunes with suggested chords and make their own arrangements of them, listening first to examples of performers in relevant styles.

A further possibility arising from this work is that of extending it to electric instruments as a pop or rock band format, preserving more or less the same roles.

focus on

- ability to learn, memorise and improvise material;
- ability to fulfil appropriate musical function in a group or band;
- sense of style and appropriate performing techniques.

mixed groups

It is often possible to form small ensemble groups of children learning instruments who can enjoy working together over a longer stretch of time and investigate later the possibilities of composing for the group. For instance, in the summer, the first half-term of rehearsal times for a junior school orchestra were set aside for improvisation and composition work in small groups. The instruments available included violins, 'cello, recorders, flutes, clarinets and tenor horn. The activities they undertook are described here as examples only and can be adapted for any small groups of players. There is no need for a teacher organising such work to have knowledge of how to play each instrument. If technical help is needed, instrumental teachers can be referred to, but on the whole the children work easily on their own within their technical capabilities. The teacher's main function is to organise, break work down into stages, listen, give feedback and focus learning.

~ In groups, think about and discuss ways of beginning pieces for a small group of players.

> After listening to a piece by Gorecki, these children worked in threes and fours improvising beginnings which started in a very quiet sustained, thin-textured way and built up gradually, though using only a very few notes. Listening to these openings and thinking about them afterwards showed many different ideas for using texture and not just dynamics to build up. In some of the music, instruments joined one at a time, using either the same or different melodic ideas. Three flutes started together and moved together all the way through but still made the music sound as if it was building up. This required a lot of control of dynamics and tone and intensity through embouchure and breathing.

~ Think about texture itself and the different ways a composer can use three or four players.

> Some of the children's groups had been of the same instrument e.g. the flutes, others were mixed. There was discussion about the pros and cons for a composer of using a group of all one instrument or a group of mixed instruments or mixed sizes e.g. of recorders. What problems does either arrangement give you? What opportunities? Children's

comments on groups of like instruments included:

'it's difficult because you've got the same sound all the time' *(timbre)*
'it's easier because different instruments are in different keys' *(working out transposing instruments)*
'it's good because you're going to know that they're going to go together' *(timbre)* and 'that they could do the same things as each other if you wanted them to' *(range and technique)*
'you could know if they're doing the right notes' (if all are also playing the same tune).
In favour of a mixture was:
'it's good because you've got different sounds and because some instruments are higher and some are lower' *(timbre and pitch)*.

The Cornish composer, Graham Fitkin, has been interested in homogenous ensembles, for example, writing pieces for up to six pianos. The children listened to the opening sections of two of his pieces, first *Hook*, for four percussionists playing four marimbas or four sets of rototoms, played by Ensemble Bash, and then *Stub* for four saxophones, played by Delta Saxophone. Comments included:
Hook
'It's got a mixture of sound – high and low – and it's very fast.'
'Jumpy.'
'It's good because it's the same tune (rhythm) all the way through but it just uses different pitches.'
Stub
'Very jumpy.'
'When they all played the notes they didn't exactly go together' (dissonant).
'It reminds me of people rushing about everywhere.'
'Busy.'
'Quite loud.'
'It sounds like the music of a spooky film.'
The last comment on *Hook* was the one used for trying out in groups.

In a group of the same instruments, make a beginning for a piece where everyone plays the same rhythm, keeping together, although they might use different tunes or pitches. In other words, this is an exploration of homophonic texture, in which all instruments move together.

Sameness of sound in some ways e.g. timbre highlights the use of other kinds of structures e.g. pitch and rhythm and this seems to be what interests this composer. Borrowing the opening ideas of these two pieces, beginning with rhythmic unity, posed the problem of how to use the pitch space in melody.

Among these children's pieces there were examples of:

- a unison syncopated rhythm, alternating groups of three and four beats, with the melodies moving in parallel direction, five notes and octaves apart;
- a three-time unison rhythm, moving up and down the notes of a chord, while one instrument played a melody line over the top;
- starting one at a time, with different pitches and timbres, then adding doubled notes into the basic rhythm, so same but different;
- a quaver rhythm in four time, slurred and breathed identically, gradually developing into a new rhythm, but with all moving on a chord in parallel harmony.

Any of these plans can be explored further or compared to music by other composers.

In the same groups, make a piece which works with textures in which players move at different times and not everyone is playing all the time.

As with any investigative approach to listening and composing the possibilities multiply as each new experience gives rise to further questions.

| focus on | - understanding of different ways of using instruments in a small group composition;
- listening skills used in developing the music;
- imaginative ideas in composing or interpreting and ability to realise these with performers. |

Listening skills

Listen to musical examples and try to describe the way instruments are treated either as individuals or as a group. Think about how this has been done through melody, rhythm and timbre.

Listen to music for three clearly different instruments. Ask three children to follow a line each, standing when 'their' instrument is playing and sitting when it stops. This could be developed into more quality dance work if a larger space is available. Keep a watching group to describe what they see.

Listen to an example of music with clear harmony (not moving too fast). Indicate each time you hear the chord change. How often are the changes? Discuss the effects of the changing chords and pick out particularly noticeable changes.

| focus on |

- the different textures created by varying numbers of players and how they are combined in a group;
- the harmonic effects of combinations of pitched instruments.

individual progression

Each child builds up their experience and skills in instrumental playing gradually but steadily through the 7–11 age phase. More than this though, the hope is that each child has the opportunity to begin to establish instrumental playing as an aspect of their own musical identity, either by concentrating hard on a single instrument or by trying different instruments and roles in different performing groups. For some children, the main motivation may be in preparing and performing for audiences; others may want to avoid this. For some, the interest may be more in using this experience towards composing; or performing may be subsumed into electronic music making where the performance is laid down in memory and worked with so that the final 'product' is on tape or disc. Some children will find it easier to learn for short concentrated periods of time towards very specific occasions or outcomes e.g. taking part in a show or performing a peer composition to the class. Some may develop their skills entirely within their own self-formed group e.g. a girl or boy band, a folk group, a singing duo.

assessment points

early stages

The child:
- can distinguish a range of instrumental sound, and describe the sound and how it is made;
- can compose imaginative music for single instruments, and for two players, matching the music to the instrument's capabilities;
- understands a range of ways in which music can be composed for one, two or more instruments and can talk about texture in relation to other elements;
- can perform instrumental music alone and with a partner, keeping together and listening to each other.

later stages

The child:
- can listen to music for one, two or more parts, beginning to be able to follow the lines separately and together, and describe the timbres and textures used;
- can compose imaginative music for a range of single instruments, including for another player to perform, showing knowledge of the instruments' potential and capabilities; can compose music for two or more players, making decisions based on some understanding of texture in part music;
- can appraise instrumental music by other composers, making comparisons of the different ways music for one, two or more parts can be structured;
- can perform instrumental music alone and in a group, showing listening and ensemble skills.

maximising
opportunities

primary music: later years

The broad organisation of music teaching for the later years of primary schooling is often left as it has always been. Teachers' immediate concerns are with what to teach and less so with rethinking the wider scope decisions of how time, people, spaces and so on are used in catering for children's music learning. Yet the structuring of music teaching presents a number of inescapable issues: vital if all children are to be given maximum opportunities to make the most of their musical potential. Some of these decisions are school-wide, some of them rest with year planning groups and individual teachers: all will arise from a set of carefully defined priorities for music.

The whole class music lesson has remained as the dominant format for teaching music, surviving in much the same guise in spite of developments during recent years. Around the class lesson, music is also provided for in a number of different kinds of timetable slot, for different groupings of children, by different kinds of staffing, both in and out of the fixed school timetable day. The following list gives some idea of this range:

- timetabled lesson for a single class: *once or twice a week;*
- hymn practice for year group or whole school: *once a week;*
- assembly – singing and listening to music: *daily;*
- classroom-based individual, group and whole class work; *time allocation and frequency varies;*
- lunchtime or after-school sessions for specific activities, music clubs, folk dancing etc: *once a week;*
- special musical events, whole school: *annual festival calendar;*
- lessons for learning instrumental or voice skills – individual or small group: *once a week.*

Reading through this list it seems clear that primary schools are places where much music is happening in a climate which recognises that music has particular requirements of people and time. Primary schools have the advantage of being small organisations where small groups of people are used to adapting quickly, to pooling abilities and to becoming 'multi-skilled'. They can allow for considerable flexibility over the way in which time, space and people are used, even though it may at times feel otherwise. So, there is, in primary schools, a good basis from which the broad organisation of music can be re-thought. This does not necessarily imply providing more from already stretched resources but using a set of defined priorities to determine how what resources there are might be used more effectively to provide the best musical opportunities for children. At the same time, it should be born in mind that the more teachers work successfully within inadequacies, the less need there may appear to be for authorities to provide more and better. Coping with what is should not mean losing sight of what ought to be.

As hopes and aims for music teaching develop into practical action the going gets tougher. Some of the priorities which define these hopes and aims have already been explored in earlier sections on listening awareness and imagination. These are the kinds of 'mind work' which are central to music learning. Although difficult to achieve in non-purpose accommodation with large classes, to compromise is to lose the very qualities which make music what it is. As a pillar principle for guiding organisational decisions, trying to allow each child the space to listen and pursue their own ideas will probably highlight shortcomings and frustrations in the way music is planned for – children working in group and class music-making, for example, in contrast to allowing children to pursue their own work in music alone. The process of setting out priorities for children's music learning is continued in this chapter and is extended into thinking how these priorities might shape the broad organisation of music. Three areas are considered in turn:

● maximising opportunities;
● individual learning;
● whole class learning.

This is followed by a section which takes a practical look at the implications of all that is said in terms of planning to make time for music.

musical opportunities

It is during these middle years of childhood from 7-11 that many of the musical interests, enthusiasms and skills which develop into adulthood have their starting points. The child sings in a choir, dances with a group, hears a particular style of music on recordings, takes part in a workshop, a performance or is given an opportunity to have lessons on an instrument. Something takes a hold and develops into a lifelong musical interest, an essential part of the child's and adult's musical personality and way of identifying themselves musically to the world. It can even, for some, be pinpointed to one inspirational moment.

So it is crucial that there are many and varied musical starting points available to all children during these years and that the first stages of encouragement and setting off are built in primary schooling. The 7–11 age phase represents a window of opportunity. Children of this age are quick to learn new skills; new coordinations connecting hand and eye and ear will develop with relative facility. These are the same children who will practise for hours with balls, ropes, roller-blades or whatever the latest craze, and can use this capacity for learning music and dancing skills. Their ability to concentrate and remember has increased since the early years so that they can tackle new and challenging learning tasks with some independence for longer periods of time. Most 7–11 year olds are receptive and open-minded, not yet held back by the cautions of early adolescence.

Schools provide musical opportunities; there is singing, playing instruments, dancing, recorder club, choir, instrumental tuition and so on. But it may be that access to many of these is limited to groups of chosen children, or groups who self-select. Ensuring that there is enough range to catch up all children may need a cool hard look at what is provided and how it is made available to children. It may well be that the instrument, the kind of activity, the style of music is not suited to the child, rather than assuming that the child is not suited to what the school offers. By the age of eleven it is not uncommon to find some children who have threaded their way through most of the musical opportunities they encountered. They were the ones who sung, took part in the performances, played the recorder, took advantage of the flute lessons and so on. In contrast a number of children will have missed or dodged most of them, reaching the end of primary schooling with a limited catalogue of musical experience behind them – that this serious discrepancy does happen is deeply troubling.

In maximising opportunities it is not suggested that an unrealistic range of musical activity is provided for. A subtle valuing of some musical experiences over others can operate so that those lower in the hierarchy may count for less. To redress the balance instantly increases the range of opportunities. In one school, for example, to attend violin 'lessons' the children were permitted to miss periods of class time whereas the guitar 'club' _as voluntary attendance during the lunch hour. A tea_her _____mally to listen and talk about a piece of music fro_ ___ _____ical tradition and on another occasion allow chil_ __ ___ ece of reggae music while they clear up. Valui_ __ ___ ll styles of music and musical processes (f_ _____ _ating notation over oral – aural methods of re_ __ _ng on music) is an essential part of fanning out _ _____ and demonstrating that there are many equa_ _____ athways to take; that there are many differ__ _____sical.

Similarly, each memb_ _____te their own way of being musical to the s_ _____he child meets adults as classteacher, lunch-tim_ _____er, office administrator, they can come into co_ _____many ways in which adults behave musically. The folk-singing teacher organises his year group work around this skill while the drum-kit playing teacher is given a timetabled slot for her to work with groups of children over a six week period. The school administrator talks enthusiastically to children about songs she remembers and organises a listening session from her old record collection. Around this framework of pooled skills and enthusiasms, other adults can add to and fill-in what the staff consider to be gaps in what they are providing. These music contributors might be:

- visiting instrumental teachers;
- community musicians;
- outreach project workers from orchestras, opera and dance companies;
- parents and other adults;
- pupils from secondary schools, students from higher education.

Bringing music workers into school to liaise with classteachers in providing experiences within their planning framework has the added bonus of making links with music beyond the school, into community music organisations and further afield.

In planning to ensure a rich array of musical starting points for all children teachers face dilemmas. They have a real duty to enable children to find themselves in the music of school so that they can musically connect their worlds of home, community and school. Providing a set of steelpans or organising workshops of Khatak dance may be ways in which schools decide to relate to the musical backgrounds of their children. Yet teachers will also wish to expand and broaden musical horizons. Providing opportunities will involve a careful balance of respect and appreciation of children's home culture with an understanding of the ever-present biases which accompany gender, race and physical ability and working to compensate. It may be even more important, for example, that schools provide lessons on Western instruments for children who may otherwise miss out. Similarly, finding ways to break with stereotypes of gender so that, say, boys don't balk at singing or girls shy from taking the lead part on the largest drum is one more aspect of maximising opportunities.

In ensuring a range of opportunities for all children, the teacher will have a management, co-ordinating and monitoring role. Music notebooks in which the children can track experiences both within and without school can help a teacher to see where connections can be made or gaps are emerging. For some children ways in to music are provided by parents or community groups. The teacher helps the child to use and make connections between these out-of-school experiences and in-school work. This might mean more than, say, a child bringing tabla drums in to school to perform in assembly but might involve preparing a composition with others for tabla and recorders or borrowing a number of CDs of virtuoso players to investigate performance styles. For other children who have little out of school musical opportunity teachers will want to ensure that the school provides. Conversations with the child, other staff, parents and visiting teachers will help the teacher to build up a picture of the child across all their musical activity. In this way the teacher can ensure that by the final stage of primary school all children will have threaded their way through a fair spread of experiences and that every effort has been made to overcome inequities of opportunity.

individual learning

Seeing children as musicians in their own right, just as we are accustomed to seeing them as individual writers or artists or dancers, is essential in raising expectations and improving the quality of musical experience and outcomes. Whilst this can happen to some extent within classwork, the significance of giving children regular opportunities to work alone in music throughout this age-phase cannot be underestimated.

Why does this even need saying? No one imagines that children could develop as writers if they only ever worked in groups or planned pieces of whole-class writing. No one expects children to produce all their art-work jointly by agreeing decisions with five others, or to paint side by side on part of a shared 'canvas'. Group activity of this kind in English or art is occasional and supports individual development; it couldn't possibly encompass it.

Why can music be different? A ready answer to this might be that music is very often made in groups, with numbers of players and singers together. We could go further and say that this social aspect of music is one of the reasons we value it so highly in our communities and in education. Culturally, however, we are, for better or worse, far down a road of perceiving music as a matter for individual creativity and response as well as for group participation. In many musical styles, composing, improvising, performing and even listening are practised on a basis of individual work as much as of a shared responsiveness. Given this to be so, to expect children to learn music in entirely communal contexts seriously undermines large parts of their musical development. Such practice adopts the social nature of musical performance as the basis for an educational practice – that of learning music by making it and listening to it together. This works for some aspects of individual music learning but not for others.

There really is a parallel between the inappropriateness of asking children to write or draw only in groups and asking them to compose only in groups. There is as much difficulty in practising instrumental performing skills and interpretation without any time alone as there is in practising writing or drawing skills in similar circumstances. It is strange to expect children to learn music without ever inventing or listening and responding to, or making judgments about, music for themselves, by themselves. In music, working alone is a necessary complement to working with others. Both are important and they are different.

The experiences of taking a yacht around the world single-handed, even for the first time taking the wheel of a boat on the river estuary, must offer an order of recognition of oneself in the world and of steering according to one's own judgment, entirely different from the experience of being carried along as one of a crew. There are some aspects of learning music which demand that a core of working alone is sustained, around which the rest of music learning activity is planned.

If children are to have the opportunity to develop a sense of their own musical creativity, time alone is needed for composing or performing activity in which they are able to draw on their inner listening sense. They need to get the feel of what it is *like* to choose, decide, shape and make music according to their own uninterrupted stream of musical alertness, sensitivity, inventiveness and response. This sense can be very fragile to begin with and it easily disappears in a group situation. Children who can play (in the other sense, recreationally) alone have a head start in this, being used to evolving imaginatively as they go along, guiding events according to an inner world of imagination.

The physical and aural skills involved in music-making need practising alone as well as in a group situation. Children need to hear themselves play and sing alone, listen to the sound and adjust it accordingly. They need to practise it in their own time, at their own speed. They need to try out techniques, repeat parts over and over again, and hear the consequences. They need to build their own level of physical fitness – of finger, voice, body or breath control – and stamina. They need to keep fit and move on to more challenging levels. We have a general understanding that this is necessary for anyone learning an instrument in formal lessons; but this understanding is not widely enough applied to all children in each class as they try to develop vocal and instrumental skills on a range of instruments.

Working alone allows children to choose music for listening and become immersed in it by themselves. This removes the demands usually present in a group listening situation to focus on specified aspects or to respond or discuss the music in particular ways. Storr (1992), in his exploration of music in relation to the human psyche, points out that 'the solitary listener to music depends upon modern technology and is therefore historically a newcomer.' He goes on to ask:

> *Has music's function changed because it is no longer necessarily shared? Or does the possibility of experiencing music in solitude simply clarify and underline its effects upon the individual listener?*

These are questions which can usefully be discussed with children. Whatever view one holds, however, beyond school solitary listening is a readily available and widely used form of musical experience – from the bedtime tapes played on a child's machine to music collections played on personal stereos and hi-fi. It is to be expected then, that children in school will be encouraged to borrow music from a listening library and widen their listening tastes and skills just as they will be borrowing books. Individual listening can be linked to opportunities for children to develop their own appraising and response by writing or taping critical reviews or through creative writing, art, dance or video.

making opportunities for working alone

The main reasons why individual work is often missing from primary school provision for music are much more likely to do with history and practicalities than rooted in any educational objections. It is probably not too contentious to suggest that giving children the opportunities suggested above immediately raises the level of their work and their motivation too.

Practically, the idea of children working alone can be initially daunting. First, the issue of sound arises – both the sound made by children's work and the need for a quiet enough space for them to hear what they are doing. Whereas a whole class can be writing or painting, working alone but all at the same time, with music each individual ideally needs their own sound space. This is quite a challenge. Second, though connected, is the fact that some schools have packaged up their music teaching into single lesson slots once a week, possibly even taught by a visiting, part-time teacher. This is very problematic, since it precludes the flexibility for individual opportunities and usually means that parts of the music curriculum are omitted altogether.

In planning to provide opportunities for each child to work alone in music, the following points can be considered:

- children will need to take turns; they can't all work alone at once;
- plan long term: look for a spread of opportunities for each child over the year;
- opportunities can be different for each child; not everyone needs to do everything;
- sort out the kind of activities which need frequent turns from those which can be blocked much less frequently; sort also according to equipment needed and noise-level;
- include working at lunchtimes or during after school activity times as a possibility;
- include working at home, whether voluntary or as 'homework';
- consider how to balance opportunities which are scheduled with opportunities 'on demand';
- review current resource provision (e.g. of listening equipment, CDs and tapes, instruments and technology) in relation to working alone as well as classwork; adjust the perspective;
- review how the school might provide for work alone in music, including visiting helpers who might staff additional spaces for such work;
- recognise that all music activity requires quiet.

The following examples show a range of ways to provide for particular kinds of work alone:

- Listening centre CD/tape with headphones or personal stereo for listening to choices of music. Access to collection of recorded music – both professional and recordings of children's work. Provision for different ways of appraising and for investigation/information. *Choosing and listening; forming own judgments; heightening awareness of own thoughts and responses; writing or appraising in other ways. Comparing performances, learning from other performers or composers. Gathering ideas for own work. Pursuing investigations.*

- Time and place to practise on an instrument or voice learned in a group or individual lesson, or introduced in class. Focus might be given through a practice diary with entries by pupil and teacher (see: music notebooks page 182), or by recording work and listening back to it. *A mixture of skill practice and opportunity to try individual interpretations of music and to add new pieces to repertoire, perhaps pieces composed by self or a friend; to practise parts for group music and hear clearly.*

- Xylophone, metallophone or glockenspiel, available to one child at a time to use in classroom at specified times. Chromatic (i.e. with sharps and flats as well) if possible. Range of mallets provided. *For composition; for learning and practising solo melodic music or parts for work in a group later; improvising using different note sets. Might be used for working out and playing melodies from pitch notation or standard notation.*

- Keyboard or drum machine with headphones for individual use. *For composing or performing work as above; with added facility of being able to record and save work, use playback, mix pre-set backings with live performance.*

Provision for working alone may be an aspect of music which will need to be introduced gradually over time. The difference it makes to children's attainment and motivation more than makes up for any initial difficulties of reorganising to make it possible.

whole class music

To start from a basis of real concern for pupils' individual learning in music begins to change the nature of learning music in whole class settings. The most effective music teaching is likely to result from a combination of individual and group work integrated with whole class learning.

Instead of seeing a class for music as a complete unit in which all children take part in roughly the same way with roughly the same outcomes, the teacher now sees a class of thirty or so individual learners. This change of view goes hand in hand with a clear understanding that learning in music is not simply acquired by taking part. If music is seen as a practical activity involved only with natural ability and some skill development, then expectations will remain low. An emphasis upon content and simple didactic learning processes, for example, learning a song by rote, remembering the melody and words, 'getting it right' through repetition, seriously neglects the imaginative and creative side and the child's real understanding of things musical. An emphasis upon process, as, for example, in certain kinds of composing activity can lead to busy, hands-on activity on the part of the child but light-weight results. In-depth learning will emerge from involvement in musical ideas, not just doing but children listening perceptively and imaginatively, analysing, investigating and in all kinds of ways exercising their musicality (Sugrue, 1997). Essential in achieving this is the teacher's role in setting up interactive situations of listening, discussing, pondering, challenging and deciding. Children become equal partners with the teacher in special kinds of music teaching and learning communications, exchanges both musical and verbal in which ideas are bandied about – talk, constantly pausing to listen attentively to the music which is its focus, and the music pausing to allow for thinking and sharing of thoughts.

This kind of talking and listening partnership between teacher and children can be perpetuated in whole class sessions which follow on from or lead in to individual or group working. Whole class working is not something separated out from working alone but connected to it. Class gatherings may be a time when threads of individual work are brought to a forum in which all children are involved in a process of listening, talking and deciding on next stages. All children can gain from the process of listening in or contributing to discussion. On other occasions the whole class time may be an opportunity to teach skills or give information and instructions in a time-saving and energy-saving way. Whole class routines are, on one level, simply efficient ways of teaching. The children can then go on to use these instructions, information and skills in their own lines of activity.

Other teaching strategies for whole class working will be teacher led but will emphasise the importance of engaging children actively in processes of musical thinking and thinking about their own learning. This is likely to involve a careful appraisal of the forms of talking and questioning which the teacher uses. At the same time, these strategies will make space for children's individual threads of activity. Lessons will be guided by clear learning goals but remain flexible to children's individual contributions. Much of this happens in a climate of joint discovery, a kind of uncertainty for what might happen which makes the 'what next?' absolutely exciting. This does not allow for the slapdash, nor an over-dependence on just the children's ideas. But behind does lie a real trust of the child's ability and imagination, if challenged, prodded and guided, to produce children's music work of quality and vitality. Sensitive and lively communication, both verbal and musical, encourages the child to take the initiative, setting high standards and respecting each child for their individuality.

models of whole class working

The whole class lesson with children gathered around the piano for singing is perhaps so familiar to all as representative of school music that alternative models of music teaching are difficult to imagine. To have the whole class for half an hour or more is a difficult and tiring way to teach music, often complex if more is attempted than the simplest of rote routines. Communal piano-led singing may be the best way of coping with a crowd. It is orderly and sends a familiar sound into the corridors of the school. Making changes may appear to carry no convincing gains. Pictures of alternative class music sessions are described below. Much of this is simply about bringing in processes of teaching which are good practice in any area. In each of the snapshots the rate of music-making activity has slowed down – and quietened down – but the learning goes deeper, focusing in rather than moving on.

The first collection looks at children bringing individual activity to a whole class forum. It took place with a class of children who spanned both Years 5 and 6.

● The class have assembled around the classroom computer and two children are explaining how they have worked out part of their composition using a program which the class has recently acquired. The teacher asks that they demonstrate slowly some of the processes so that other children can learn from them.

Listening carefully, the teacher sometimes intervenes to clarify, ask extending questions or to summarise what the children have said and to ensure that all the children listen carefully to the music which results. *A 'present and tell' session of work which was in progress encourages the children to clarify their ideas so that they can explain to others. It benefits the rest of the children in the class who can learn from their information giving. Expertise acquired by some children can move the whole class forward if it is shared in this way.*

- Four children who have been working independently on separate compositions during the week are invited to bring work in progress to a class forum. The pieces are played in turn and everyone listens. Next the teacher discusses aspects of their work with each of the four composers in turn while the rest of the class listen in. *Children listening to one another's work, even though they are not directly involved, is one source for gathering ideas for their own work. Being party to the discussion between teacher and child in which the music is described and evaluated models for all children the process of talking about music, the kinds of vocabulary to use and the process of evaluating music.*

- Over a period of a whole term the class has been involved in a song composing project. Many of the finished songs were performed to parents and other adults at the end of term. The teacher holds a session to review the term's work with the children, talking with them about what they had learnt, how this fitted in with their progress over a longer period of time and what they might move on to next. *Thinking about learning and being able to chart progress, identifying what they have achieved and what they can now go on to, is important in children becoming independent learners.*

This second group of snapshots looks at ways in which the teacher uses strategies for whole class work which make room for individual contributions:

- The teacher composes a melody on a keyboard while the class listen in. She models the process. First the keyboard settings must be decided. The children give her suggestions and these are tried out. The tempo and overall character of the melody she will make is discussed. As the melody is worked out the teacher gives a running commentary on the process of finding ideas, rejecting some, fixing others and so on, inviting dialogue between herself and the children. *The teacher acts out the processes of composing for the children to learn from. She has technical skills on the instrument beyond the children's capabilities so they are able to hear their suggestions immediately transformed into musical ideas.*

● The class has decided that they would like to learn a song which they have chosen from a book and tape in the music area. The teacher takes the lead in teaching the class to remember the words and melody of the song, using both the taped version and her own live-singing version. When the song is known, the children are set the task of working on the song, experimenting with ideas on tempo, vocal timbre, dynamics and styles of ornamentation. They disperse in pairs into the space of the hall and sing quietly to themselves. The class re-assembles to listen to different singings of the song and interpretations are discussed. *In this way the teacher makes room for the children to contribute their own ideas in the paired work.*

The two descriptions above also attempt to break the usual molds of grouping and working for the activities of composing, performing and listening. The kind of working pattern often used for composing, setting up an activity and sending away small groups to work on a given idea is here applied to a singing performance activity. Likewise, composing which is often managed as a small group activity is here taught in a whole class format with the teacher taking a lead role. If we accept that the style of teaching interaction will have a profound influence on the nature and quality of children's learning, then it is important to look again, critically, at usual ways of structuring teaching.

Such questions also lead into a evaluation of how time is allocated for children's learning.

time

How much do we expect children to learn over a period of time? Many children are hurried in their music learning and are denied generously long stretches of time in which to broaden and deepen their involvement in one thing – nothing large and complicated can happen. If music is only visited once a week for a fixed time slot there is little incentive to become involved in tasks which may soon have to finish and will not be taken up again until next week. Children can only make proper use of experiences if they have time to learn, reflect and respond on their own terms. Being able to stay with, repeat, continue and consolidate music activity is more likely to result in real motivation and learning – and result in music work of real sensitivity and imagination. Given kinds of 'elastic time' opportunities, each child has more of a chance to find what holds their interest and develop it.

Different kinds of musical activity are best catered for in different timespans. There are some kinds of learning, developing skills in particular, which may be best practised in frequent, short bursts of time. At this end of the time scale, a quick-fire aural game at the computer may be most effective in turns of five minutes each. In contrast, intensive workshop sessions of long afternoons may precede a performance occasion being prepared by the whole class together. On a year plan for music, this bout of intensive workshop activity may then be balanced by a period when other forms of music activity requiring lighter timetable provision come to the fore. Organisation of the timetable might start with an overview of the whole year in which patches of time are planned in. This is, after all, only a version of what happens already for music but in an unsaid way – everyone knows that the end of the Autumn term is likely to mean long rehearsal periods in preparation for an end of term performance – or that the timetable of the visiting teacher will cause a change of music teaching patterns in the Spring term. A change of emphasis and priority guides the broad organisation of music so that priorities defined by what will create best learning opportunities for children determine how the time, spaces and people are distributed. It might result in a small shift in how resources are actually used but behind lies a huge shift in thinking and emphasis.

This is what a year plan might begin to look like:

- 2 intensive weeks, whole class projects to prepare music drama/music and dance performances: a once yearly festival event;
- a half term of individual work, composing activity: *one half term throughout the year, visiting parent to help;*
- six week 'module' of instrumental skills input, whole class in rota groups: *planned around availability of visiting teacher;*
- half term set of whole class lessons for music and dance: *once a week, shared with other teacher for same year group;*
- 15 minute whole class music circle times to keep track of singing work: *most of the year;*
- lunchtime or after-school club opportunities to practise instruments or take part in composing groups: *organised on a rota with other teachers across key stage, lunchtime assistants, after-school club workers help organise rota;*
- half term of music program on computer (planned to tie in with topic) work in pairs: *turns in pairs across week, work gathered up in whole class session at end of week;*
- 10/15 minute listening times at listening centre (two at a time with headphones): *on a long-running rota system according to register;*
- series of ten minute 'input' sessions to teach basic singing skills and play music games: *first weeks of Autumn term with new class;*
- 'spot' whole class lessons to give 'lead from' information or skill input; *occasionally, as necessary;*
- one-off workshops, concerts given by visiting musicians; *occasionally.*

Each of the sets of investigations in the practical work sections of this book includes a preliminary section called 'planning points'. Here suggestions are given for the kinds of timetable slot which might be planned for in keeping with this discussion on maximising musical opportunities for all children.

music, dance
and drama

This section focuses on the integration of music with dance, words and drama. The common ground shared by each with music allows children to develop the particular musical skills and understanding which belong to the context of each art form. The learning that arises also feeds back into an understanding and practice of music in its own right. The first part looks at the connections between dance and music and at teaching and learning approaches in which they are combined. The second part suggests a series of practical investigations based on traditional dances from different parts of Europe. These investigations aim to model approaches for working with dance and music as a springboard for teachers' own planning. In addition, these ideas for working with traditional dances present some approaches for investigating music of other places. The third section suggests practical activities which explore ways of bringing together music, words and drama in different contexts. These offer very varied opportunities in which to apply vocal and instrumental performing skills and to learn to compose within the constricts which text or drama impose.

music and dance

Every one of us recognises the almost irrepressible desire to move when the music takes hold. Both dance and music are rooted in sensations of timing and rhythm, intensity and dynamics which we feel in the physical activity of our body. In dance these fundamental sensations are transformed into movements which we see and feel kinaesthetically; in music they are transformed into the medium of sound which we hear and also, in some ways, feel physically. Dance and music are two dimensions of the same bodily feelings so that music in this sense is a kind of audible dancing and dance a kind of silent music. Because of these connections, each can be readily translated into the other. Sometimes, for example, we find ourselves describing the music with a series of gestures when words are not enough or enhancing dance movements with vocal syllables and sounds. This process of translating back and forth and so gaining a physical insight into the music and an audible insight into the dance can be used to the benefit of music learning of every kind and at all ages.

So it becomes difficult to imagine teaching music and dance in ways that do not recognise the one embedded in the other. During the early years of primary schooling the importance of movement in music teaching is well recognised but as children move into the later years of primary schooling, it is fair to say that the connections between music and dance are underestimated and under-used. Developing an awareness and sensitivity to the movement dimensions and qualities of music is vital in all musical experience, whatever the age being taught and whatever the nature of the musical activity. To begin to think carefully about the contribution of dance to music education in the later years of primary schooling, the ways in which dance and music integrate are generalised below in four categories:

- dance listening;
- investigating dances of time and place;
- movement and music activities which focus on elements;
- choreography.

The sections which follow now look at these four categories of learning approach in more detail.

dance listening

When children dance to music, either dancing a set dance or improvising free dance, their listening sensitivity, concentration and musical memory become intrinsically connected to the physical acting out of the music in time and in space. This is what is meant by 'dance listening' (Loane, 1984). The activity of dancing the music requires children to convert what they hear into movements which match or complement the music and if they are to do this well they must be aurally alert and physically responsive.

Musical understanding relies to a large extent upon the ability to remember and relate what has happened 'before' and 'after' in the music; in other words, to be able to place what has been listened to and remembered across a span of time. Dancing helps children to listen for and locate musical moments and to understand the relationships between these events. So, for example, by dancing a folk dance, knowing when and becoming aware of the musical moment to change direction and turn back for each phrase becomes attached to the steps and formations of the dance. There is something particularly impressionable and memorable about using your body to do exactly as the music does.

Dancing is such an intense experience, exciting and arousing, that it can detract from listening, particularly if children have little prior experience of dance listening to music. With youngest children teachers' first concerns will be to ensure that children focus their listening attention upon the music and match their movements to what they hear – the dance listening activity may need to proceed with moments of quiet, inactive listening alternating with movement. Older children with more experience of dancing to music will be able to focus their attention and in repeat hearings work on detailed choreographies from which they will gain a particular insight into the workings of the music.

investigating dances of time and place

People of all cultures dance and have danced at all times in the past. By taking part in the dances of other times and places something of those cultures is absorbed. To lift the ribcage, push the shoulders back and raise the arms for one of the dances of the flamenco tradition is to feel immediately a body style which is unfamiliar to northern Europeans. Compare this dance style with the slow, restrained movements of Japanese dance or the athletic virtuosity of Russian Cossack dancing and one can come to understand how learning dances as an integral part of learning a musical style adds a vital dimension which cannot be gained from inactive listening alone.

To complement their movements dancers stamp, clap, click, sing or play portable instruments, or they bring in players and singers to make music. The music made absorbs the tempo, rhythm patterns, dynamics, form and qualities of the dancers' style of dancing. If there are many dancers moving together the music helps all to move in synchrony by giving a strong pulse and by indicating the points of change in the dance steps and formations. Dance and music have a strong reciprocal effect on one another – live music played for dancing will catch from the dancers and vice versa. Indeed, it may be impossible and completely out of keeping with the music/dance traditions of certain cultures to separate out music from the dance – as for example in music/dance traditions from different regions of the African continent (Kwami, 1986).

Other dance musics are 'detachable' from the bodily movements of the dance itself and can take on a life of their own away from the dancers. Some can be either danced to or listened to, as in much pop music or folk dance music. Other kinds of dance music have broken loose from their dancing origins entirely and were – or are – written only for playing and listening to. The physical movements of the dance provide the composer with a blueprint of rhythmic patterns and structures, mood and character but the intention is to make a dance of music for listening to. Many of the pieces written for instruments by Western European composers fall into this category: Baroque suites, for example which are collections of dances such as minuets, sarabandes, gavottes, gigues written for several kinds of instrument groupings.

So dance and music forms range from those which are inseparable to those which have taken on a new life as independent music forms. Yet no dance musics, however distant their original dance connections, can be understood fully without knowing something of the dance itself. Take for example the minuet, a dance form in which hundreds of pieces were written for keyboard instruments, small instrumental groups and orchestras.

activity

The minuet is a dance in three time and yet the basic steps fall into a kind of two beat pattern which creates a cross rhythm effect:

- Step forward with the right foot for the first beat and bring the left foot up to the right foot instep on the second beat, bending both knees gently outward.

- Straighten the knees and during the rise, step forward with the left foot and bring the right foot against the left instep, again bending both knees gently.

- Straighten the knees and take two steps forward for the two final beats – onto the ball of the right foot and then the left foot.

The body must be held tall and straight, with the arms held gently outwards. The wrists and fingers decoratively curved and lower legs and feet turned out and pointed. (Cohen, 1992)

The basic step pattern takes up six beats; two bars of music grouped in threes and three sequences of steps grouped in twos:

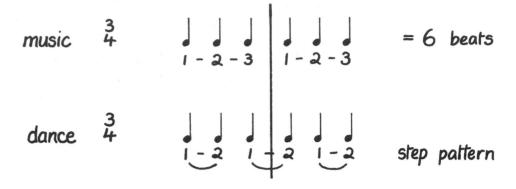

music $\frac{3}{4}$ ♩ ♩ ♩ | ♩ ♩ ♩   = 6 beats
                   1 - 2 - 3 | 1 - 2 - 3

dance $\frac{3}{4}$ ♩ ♩ ♩ | ♩ ♩ ♩
                   1 - 2   1 - 2   1 - 2   step pattern

Having danced the minuet the cross rhythm pull 'gets into the body' and thereafter subtly effects the way the minuet is performed and listened to.

Traditions in the way music is taught have tended to overlook and ignore the close connections between music and dance preferring to study, think and write about music only as if it were separated. To investigate dance musics it is essential that children are involved not only in listening to the music but in dancing and learning about dance style. Here are some of the areas they might explore:

● the ways in which music relates to dance historically and across cultures, e.g. understanding whether they are working with a bonded dance/music form or a dance music which is intended for listening alone;

● the historical, cultural and social background that informs the characteristics of style shared by both dance and music, *e.g. understanding the difference between court dances and country dances in the Tudor period;*

● the relationship between the musical form and the dance form, *e.g. looking at the difference between music and dance improvised by one dancer and player, as in flamenco, and music and dance for a large number of dancers all moving together;*

● the different groups of players and singers who make music for dance, *e.g. single whistler, a band playing traditional instruments of Bulgaria, an orchestra of Western classical instruments, electro-acoustic music pre-recorded;*

● how the dance fits into the life of the community, *e.g. is this an everyday social dance, a dance for special occasions, celebrations, religious purposes?*

For investigating dance musics, descriptions of dances with photos can go some way, for example, the reproduced pictures and diagrams of dance steps from *The Art of Dancing* by Kellom Tomlinson published in 1735 and re-printed in 1972 for studying historical dance. But for investigating contemporary dancing video provides the ideal source. Video gives a direct impression of the dance style and can be halted or replayed for study. Visiting workshop leaders, both dancers, singers and players can give children direct experience of learning and performing set dances of certain times or places, or working in specific dance styles.

movement and music activities for focused learning

Specific musical skills and aspects of learning about the musical elements can be focused on either by isolating some part of the dance and its music to spotlight a learning point or by designing music and movement exercises which have a specific learning purpose. In the second part of this section, 'Traditional Dances', a number of practical examples of such activities are given.

It is crucial that the music and dancing remain central so that the focus activities both lead from and lead back into experiences of working with complete dance and music forms. For example, dancing an Eastern European line dance may be prepared by working on a tempo activity which gives children practice at stepping *'all together in time'* with the same sized steps. The musical materials, or elements, will always be looked at in the context of specific examples of dance and music.

The sample music/movement activities connected with the investigations which follow later in this section focus on the understanding of time-based elements, those associated with musical tempo, metre, rhythmic patterning and form in European music. However, movement based-activities can be designed for focused work with time-based elements as found in other styles of music and for musical elements beyond the time-based such as pitch, timbre, texture: a few samples as starter ideas are given below. The cautionary reminder is added that covering these activities or others like them cannot, on their own, represent pockets of learning achievement, they are only useful as one component of whole musical experiences.

- Pitch relationships visualised with hand signs. *This supports children's understanding of pitch movement from one note to the next, up or down, by step, by small jump or wide jump, in their aural skill development and voice pitching development.*

- Melodic phrase shapes drawn in the air with gestures and/or whole body movements. *This activity emphasises the melodic shape in relation to concepts of high and low pitch, direction of movement, moving by step or moving by jump and the relationship of rhythmic movement to melodic movement.*

- Two different lines of melody sounding together can be stepped out in floor pathways. *This shows how the two parts are moving in relation to one another – parallel, following one another with the same pathway, crossing, interweaving etc.*

- Timbral qualities can be translated into body movement qualities. *Improvised movements in response to music as heard can be another dimension to support the understanding of and response to timbre.*

- Dynamics can be similarly captured either in muscular tension or in size of movements or a combination of the two. *Movement can provide a medium well-suited to the exploration of wide variations of dynamic. Children may lack technical skills to control wide variations in voice or instrumental skills.*

- Textural changes can be represented by solos and groups of children. *e.g. One child follows a solo player or single line of melody, groups of children follow all-play-together sections or harmonised sections.*

choreography

Dance and music are both time-based art forms and so the processes of composing music are closely allied to the processes of dance-making, choreography. Both involve designing in time; making structures of either sounds or bodily movements in which a sequence of events unfurl from beginning to end across a measured time span.

Working with measured time structures presents quite different challenges to children than, say, making a piece of visual art, a painting or a clay model, or other creative tasks such as writing or maths in which there is something of permanence to work with. No sooner has the movement or the musical idea been made than it is no longer there and the next needs to connect with and follow on. Memory skills become essential, as do mental methods for holding on to musical and dance ideas and imagining how they might evolve. It is these relationships across time, referring back to what has been and leading forward to what might come next which children must learn to manage.

Although the two media of bodily movement and sound behave very differently, each having certain potentials and certain constraints, borrowing the skills of dance making for music can enable children to transfer understandings from one media to another. As a teaching strategy for developing compositional skills dance movement holds certain key advantages:

● movement is a more concrete media than sound for children to work in;
● movement leaves a visual trace which helps to fix the sequence of events;
● both teacher and pupil can 'see' the thought processes;
● the terms and forms used in choreography are similar or the same as those used in musical composition, e.g. unison, canon, question and answer, binary, ternary.

There are some things which happen in dance more easily and naturally than in music – and vice versa. Unhampered by the technical demands of producing musical sounds, dances can often have a more bodily feeling for the rhythm and dynamics of a piece; a sense of momentum and energy which can simply get lost in trying to make the right notes. This vitality is the essence of time-based art forms and can lead to a sense of self-awareness and involvement which is an important source of motivation and of deep enjoyment.

What follows is a description of a series of music sessions with a class of Year 5 children working with their teacher, Kay Vernon, in a Brent school. They first investigated the *Chairman Dances* by Adams through dance listening using the awareness of how they danced to build an awareness of how the music had been structured. They then went on to compose their own music using dance ideas as starting points. The first lesson evolved into this plan of action:
    • improvise free dance to the music as heard for the first time;
    • repeat this several times;
    • sit and discuss the music and how the children danced, using

words and individual children's demonstrations of their dance movements;

- focus on certain key aspects of the music and the movements which they found to complement the music, in particular the change from regular rhythmic activity, to the more flowing, gentler style later in the piece;
- listen to parts of the music again without moving;
- decide on some things to try out when listening to the music again;
- discuss, try out and refine movement ideas in relation to the music, watch some individual children and groups working on ideas;
- each group dance their final version for the rest of the class as audience.

At the end of the session the children had arrived at semi-worked out dance sequences. There was something of the regular strong beat and insistent style of the music which encouraged improvised rap-style dancing on the part of the children. As Year 5 children they were bringing movement vocabulary familiar to them into this new context. Since the learning aim of the session was to use dancing as a medium to focus listening, to assist investigation and understand the music more thoroughly, the teacher steered the lesson in directions which kept the musical learning at the forefront. The children's attention was drawn to listening to the music and how this might be best interpreted in movement. On another occasion, the lesson direction might lead toward a dance learning aim and more time spent on inputting new movement vocabulary ideas and working out a completed choreography.

The finished dances were captured on video. Reviewing the video with the class enabled teacher and children to notice and comment on their work. Awareness and understanding of compositional processes can develop from involvement not only in making but also by watching dance and listening to music.

The next phase of the work occupied the next few sessions. The dance-listening process had highlighted characteristics of the music. Movements had set up a repetitive sameness for a long period of time so that when the change eventually arrived it had seemed all the more striking. The children discussed whether the effect would have been the same if the change had not been so delayed. In silence the children recalled their dance ideas and the ways in which they had moved. Using these ideas as a starting point the children choreographed short dance forms to become the working foundation for music compositions. They translated movement into music, choosing a format:

- dance and then play/sing;
- dance and play/sing simultaneously;
- dance and ask others to play/sing for you, at the same time.

On this occasion, the music pieces were then worked to a point where they could be performed as music on its own without the dances.

traditional dances

In this second section of the chapter traditional dances from different parts of Europe have been chosen as the focus for a series of investigations. There is already, in many primary schools, a tradition of children taking part in British folk dancing. The suggestions which follow aim to show how this foundation of folk dancing can be extended to offer many opportunities for using dance as a means for enriching children's music learning.

Knowing the traditional music and dances of the locality where we live provides a stepping off point for moving further afield – to the dances of another part of England, Wales, Scotland or Ireland. Children can create a dance just for their class, in their school, in their part of the city or rural area. The dance trail might then stretch out further into Europe but retains the sense that music and dance of other places belongs to groups of people in small localities. As a general rule for any work with music of other places, looking closely at one or two regions and coming to know the music, dance, storytelling, art etc. well is more beneficial than cultural tours which briefly and superficially visit many places.

In almost all the traditional dances chosen for this section it is the felt rhythms made by the steps in unison with the music which is the essence of the dance. It is said of Balkan line dances that the feet are like drum sticks working out the rhythms of the dance on the ground. These are dances of rhythmic movement designs made up of steps and groups of people dancing in formations. They are not dances of body shapes and gestures as in jazz dance or contemporary ballet styles for example. These traditional dances are for joining in with, for community feeling with friends, with the village, with the class and are generally danced outdoors or in a large hall; their purpose is to draw in participants, not to leave an audience viewing from the outside, as in theatre dance. From the musical point of view, the dances chosen here provide kinaesthetic knowledge of keeping in time at different speeds, of a variety of metres, of phrasing lengths and structures and of rhythm patterns. Running alongside the work with dances are some focus activities which lead from or lead into the ongoing dance activity and aim to isolate aspects of work with the musical elements for focus practice and consolidation.

planning points

This is a set of investigations which separates out into three main units: line dances, formation dances and foot-tapping dances. It is expected that each would provide a focus for a run of whole class lessons in the hall, perhaps over half a term. The focus activities for music and movement work on aspects of rhythm are linked to this dance work but would also offer activities for general use in connection with other planned work. There would be good opportunity to leave recordings of dance music available for children to work at communal dances during the lunch-hour or in after-school clubs. Some follow-on or lead-into work on the background context of the dances, say in the library or on the Internet, could be carried out individually or in small groups during class work times.

line dances

To hold hands and dance together in a line or circle is an ancient form of dancing bringing people of one community together in a powerful way. Every dancer steps the same foot work patterns in unison as the line edges this way and back. Many traditional children's song dances and singing games take this form and to keep an ongoing repertoire of song and dance games will make as important a contribution to children's music learning in the later years of primary schooling as in the earlier years. There are many line dances which are part of the folk dance tradition in parts of Europe today. The farandole is danced in parts of Provence in France but its origins reach back to Medieval times.

farandole

The form of the farandole is simple: it is a follow-the-leader line dance, usually skipped but it can be danced to a running step or even a brisk walking pace. As a first line dance it introduces the basic skills of matching steps with everyone else so that the dancers keep in time and 'in space' with one another, not pulling or distorting the line. The interest of the dance comes from the patterns the leader creates by twisting and turning the line of dancers, winding the line into tight mazes and knots, spiralling into snail shells and under arches. The leader must take small steps and also take care not to over-stretch the line. The last in line has the task of taking care of the tail end. Ten or twelve children in a line works best, although a whole class could join up to wend their way outdoors in a slow pace farandole of simple walking steps. (See Opie, 1985, for a chapter on 'Chains and Captives' which describes many of these line dance formations in detail and gives children's song dances which accompany them.)

The farandole can be accompanied by a song or by a single line of melody. Any song with a skipping, 6/8 meter could be suitable – the English song 'I Saw Three Ships' for example. The melody given here can be sung to a simple 'la' or other vowels sounds or played by a solo piper or violinist.

A tambour player, watching the dancers carefully, can improvise rhythms which help everyone to hear and feel the rhythm of the farandole. Skipping quickly gets tiring and changing to a walking step will enable children to step out the two beats in a bar division of the 6/8 metre. They could also find a quick running step, following each of the six beats to a bar rhythm and feel its grouping into two sets of three beats. These metrical groupings are shown in this diagram:

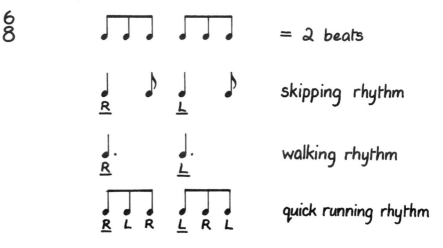

<table>
<tr><td></td><td>= 2 beats</td></tr>
<tr><td>R   L</td><td>skipping rhythm</td></tr>
<tr><td>R   L</td><td>walking rhythm</td></tr>
<tr><td>R L R   L R L</td><td>quick running rhythm</td></tr>
</table>

notice

For many children the skip poses particular coordination difficulties and to skip, sing, manage a position in a line simultaneously, adds to the possible task complexity of song-dances. Tackling each dimension separately, perhaps breaking down the skip into its component movement parts will support children's skill learning.

Having sung and danced this farandole until the melody is absorbed and the dance is rhythmically secure, children can sing their own made farandole melodies simply by improvising a sung melody as they skip or step in time. Everyone can do this at once if they sing quietly to themselves: the combined effect can be magical. This can then become the focus of a melody-making task to be continued as individual work.

The traditional folk dances of Eastern Europe are predominantly circle and line dances. The next is a line dance from Macedonia.

sletkano oro

Oro or horo simply means dance. There are hundreds of different oros, or line dances, every region having its own characteristic dances. The step-work patterns range from the simplest side steps to the most complex variations. The oldest members of the village may join in with the simple basic steps while the more energetic dance ever more complex variations.

<table>
<tr><td>activity</td><td>The step patterns given below are suggestions which use basic horo steps but are not the original steps for this dance. The children can use this given pattern or make their own versions. Once a basic step pattern has been established, children can embellish it by finding their own variations.</td></tr>
</table>

BAR 1 –   RF step to right, LF swings *behind* right foot to take next step.
RF step to right, LF closes against right foot.

BAR 2 –   Repeat in reverse:
LF step to left, RF swings *behind* left foot to take next step.
LF step to left, RF closes against left foot.

These two bars of footwork pattern and melody are repeated.

BAR 3 –   RF step to right, LF swings *behind* to take next step.
RF step to right, LF swings *in front* to take next step.

BAR 4 –   RF step to right and LF swings *behind* to take next step.
RF step to right and LF closes against right foot.

Reverse the steps of bars 3 and 4 to travel in the opposite direction to fit the two bars of repeated melody.

To learn the dance, sing the melody slowly to 'la' or other vowel sounds. A useful teaching strategy is to sing out instructions for the dance steps to the dance melody as the children are practising.

Once the steps are known the children can hold hands to dance. Hands held high, with elbows W style is characteristic of many Eastern European line dances or arms held out sideways, clasping at the shoulders. To circle is easiest at first although a line with leader and tail-ender is fun, particularly if the leader takes the line in unexpected directions and to unexpected places. The reluctance of older children to hold hands, particularly among boys, may introduce personal and social issues for discussion with the whole class.

The dancing of line dances begins at a slow, steady pace and often, as the dance progresses, the tempo gradually increases, adding to the excitement. When dancers' feet and players' fingers are moving as fast as possible with great speed and lightness, the dance finishes at a point of climax and collapse. Some other musics use the same idea of repetition combined with a gradual increase of tempo: folk music from parts of the Andes region for example. It is a structural idea, of *repeating and each time doing it a little faster* which children can experiment with in their own music work. They can:

- gradually accelerate throughout the music;
- repeat a song or short piece of played music several times and with each repetition increase the tempo;
- experiment with changes of tempo which are measured exactly to be twice as fast.

If the music is played by instrumentalists, wind instruments might take the melody line – in contemporary Bulgarian folk groups the melody is often taken by a clarinet player. Traditionally a drummer playing the tapan, a large double headed barrel drum played with thin sticks to give a dry sound, will keep a basic rhythmic pattern and will give the lead as the tempo pace increases little by little.

Listen to examples of folk music from other regions of Bulgaria, or from adjacent countries such as Greece, Albania, Roumania, Slovenia, Croatia, Bosnia-Herzegovina. Sample CDs for listening and investigating are given in the references section. Only some of the dance songs and dance musics from these places will be in the simple two-in-a-bar metre of the Oro above to which the given step pattern can be danced. Many of the line dances from Bulgaria and nearby regions have irregular beat rhythms of five, seven, nine or more beats in a bar. A way to discover these rhythms is to improvise dance steps to them – the uneven beat rhythms with their characteristic feel soon 'get into the feet'.

Here is an example of one irregular metre dance tune from Bulgaria which could be played or sung:

It is a dajchovo horo melody in which the metre has nine beats organised as:

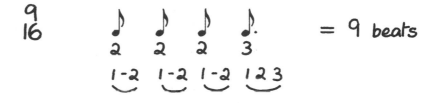

notice All of these dances make particular demands on children's ability to move in time with others and – first – maintain a steady beat at a consistent tempo and – then – to be able to control a gradual speeding up of the tempo. Look closely for how individual children are managing both.

The following section looks more closely at children's learning of tempo and suggests a set of activities which isolate the skills involved.

focus on tempo

The sense of tempo which we all carry within us, like a built-in personal timer, arises from the speed of normal walking. Each child will have their own natural pace. Some children are characteristically energetic and always rush, some are lethargic and move slowly. Personal tempo is connected deeply to personality and disposition. What we might call 'tempo disturbances' can be a clue to emotional disturbance and this is one of the points of contact between music education and music therapy. Classroom management is often, subtly, about managing the tempo of the classroom day, pacing and timing, arousing the children or calming as needs be (Woods and Jeffrey, 1996).

activity

↝ Ask one child to walk steadily at their normal tempo in and out of other children sitting on the floor in the hall. The watchers will be able to identify the walking child's normal pace as a 'moderate' speed and then identify faster, much faster, or slower, much slower without difficulty.

Having discovered individual tempi, a group of children or the whole class can attempt to settle into a common speed for walking with which they can all keep time.

This sounds like a simple process – it is not. To keep steady at our own pace is one thing, to be able to decentre and pick up a tempo outside of ourselves and then adjust to match it is a further demand. This is very similar to the difficulties children encounter in learning voice pitching skills. They may well be able to vary the pitch of their own voices quite successfully but to then adjust their singing voice to match that of others is yet more demanding. It is also similar to the difficulties some children experience in fitting in with the classroom community. Physical and emotional control are closely connected – gaining a calm control over physical movements to join in successfully with others, in a dance say, may be a major step in social adjustment.

Once progress at keeping and fitting in with tempi has been achieved, the work can move on to a wider range of tempi. Speeds which are faster or slower than our natural tempo have a psychological and physiological effect on us. Slow speeds feel calmer, soothing, lethargic, thoughtful perhaps. Fast tempi are exciting, buoyant and increase the sense of liveliness. There is a danger that school music experiences avoid the extremes of tempo. Children need the experience of working at a range of tempi to discover the effect this will have upon the mood and character of music and to discover the technical problems associated with playing, singing or dancing at very fast or very slow speeds. Children can be making careful decisions about tempo in their own performing and composing and, if scoring their work, giving written indications of tempo. Technology can enable the child to create instant tempo changes in a composition or pre-recorded performance released from possible difficulties of actually performing the music at these speeds: adjustments to tempo settings will replay recorded sections of music at various tempi.

All of these movement and music activities simply take walking as their basis. It is important that the children move with a sense of momentum and 'lift' and that the whole body is alert and responsive. If, for example, the children are stepping a phrase of 8 beats and then standing still, it is important to ensure that they move well with a sense of flow through the 8 steps and stop with control at the exact point of arrival. Taking care over the quality and precision of movement will benefit their music work; something of the same will transfer.

activities

~ Stand absolutely still and silent. Stillness and silence can have different qualities – a tense, alert stillness or a calm, relaxed stillness. Move and then stand still again. Create a sequence of movement and stillness.

~ Explore different kinds of stopping: slow down gradually to a definite stop, make a sudden 'emergency' stop, pause momentarily with a readiness to go on etc. It is unusual for music to keep going at the same speed without sometimes pausing or stopping for short moments. The music may finally end with a slowing down or a sudden stop. Explore different kinds of stop or pause in a song – a singing game such as 'The Mulberry Bush' stepped in a circle works well, but any song can be experimented with in this way. Different ways of 'stopping' may be something to listen for in all kinds of music.

↝ Each child is asked to find their own steady walking pace, using the space of the room well and not bunching or simply circulating. Walk in straight lines, curves, zig-zag shapes and trace interesting pathways. Stop and count to eight if anyone walks close to you, in front of you or you meet an obstruction. After 8 counts turn and continue in a new direction. This activity gives children practice at keeping a steady tempo and beginning to convert the kinaesthetic sensations of moving in time into an internal sense of tempo.

extensions

↝ To extend practice of the skills required in keeping a tempo: take 8 steps and stand still for the count of 8 steps at exactly the same speed. This is quite difficult as the children will tend to rush the 8 counted out steps. Individual children can practise this with a partner who helps to monitor their tempo keeping. Practise across the whole range of tempi: fast, slow.

↝ Extend the previous exercise by suggesting the children experiment with different numbers of steps and then begin to make sequences. For example, step 4 beats, count 3, step 4 beats, count 3, step 2, count 5, step 2 etc. Watch individual children step out their beat patterns and ask other children to work out number patterns by listening eyes-closed to footsteps. Fixed number sequences (best if they are not too long) could be played out on instruments and become a starting point for composition work. Working with number patterns which create uneven beat metres can relate to listening and dancing to Bulgarian dances tunes in unequal metres (see page 141).

progression

The next activities move on from learning to find and maintain a steady tempo and now tackle learning how to make changes in tempo.

activities

↝ Take one short movement pattern, say – one movement sequence from a dance, or a short gym routine, or a numbered stepping pattern – and then repeat the sequence or step pattern at a much faster or much slower tempo. 'Action replay' of sport movements is a popular activity. Pair children with one 'watcher' to comment on how accurately the speed up or slow motion version has been performed. Ask what difficulties the children encountered and discuss movement techniques which might help. For example, slow tempi always require good control of weight in making slow motion movements. Movements at fast tempi can easily lose control or tend to speed up even more.

- ～ As a whole class sit and tap knees at a very slow speed. Without anyone as leader, try gradually to get faster little by little by just listening and watching. Do this in reverse from fast to slow.
- ～ Invite individual children to start walking at their very slowest speed and little by little accelerate. This takes very careful judgment. The rest of the class watch and listen (or eyes closed and just listening to feet sounds).

Tempo changes can create musical tricks. A very fast tempo immediately before a slow tempo will alter our impression of the slow speed music making it appear even slower. The opposite also happens. Children, in their own investigations, can notice how a series of pieces often exploits this effect – for example, the sequence of songs collected together on one side of a CD or the movements of a Baroque suite.

In their own performances of European line dances the children will need to decide whether the gradual increase in tempo should be controlled by one who leads the group as a whole or can they sense when to speed up just watching and listening to one another? Will the increase be gradual or sudden? How slow should they begin? How many repetitions of the dance will they perform?

formation dances

Traditional dances of Ireland, which are made up almost entirely of jigs and reels, provide the music and dance for the next section of this chapter. Unlike the step patterns of the Balkan line dances, jigs are danced with a simple travelling step – skipping or a light running step. The interest arises from the spatial patterns created as each group of dancers line up, circle, pair off and move around the space of a hall or outdoor clearing in every kind of formation – also called 'sets' (Upton and Paine, 1996). To match the dance formations well marked out in space, the dance music is well marked out in time. Irish dance musics have a strong sense of pulse and the metre is well accented. The dance tunes fall into phrases or sections of eight bars which are then organised on the next level into sixteen and thirty two bar structures. Taking part in traditional dancing is a very valuable way to develop children's visual, kinaesthetic and aural understanding of metre, phrasing and form.

Most of the traditional instrumental music of Ireland is dance music. There are thousands of melodies for reels and jigs, originally played by a single piper, whistler or fiddler. Now only a few traditional players perform alone. Groups of players will play the single melody line together, creating a thicker, richer texture often adding the exact melody line at a lower pitch (an octave below). Some players add decorations to the melody. Although chordal backing is not the traditional Irish style, many modern groups now play with added instruments which play backings of chords. Altan is one such group playing in this more contemporary style. Much Irish music has become partially detached from its dancing origins, retaining the energy and forms of dance music but intended as much for listening to as dancing.

●———————————————————————————————————

Fiddle Sticks

Fiddle Sticks is a recording of a festival of fiddling which took place in Donegal in 1991. It provides a sampler of traditional fiddle music from this part of Ireland. There is no one Irish style; regional styles and ways of interpreting music are diverse. And individual performers will develop their own performance styles, keeping traditions alive by constantly developing and changing their music. Tommy Peoples, playing at this festival, is one of the best known fiddlers from County Donegal.

listen to

Tommy Peoples' solo performance of 'Two Jigs' (track 4). The following sequence of actions in simple formations is suggested for 'dance listening' to these jigs. The movements are simple enough for instant learning so that the children's concentration can be focused upon careful listening and will not be distracted by complicated movements. The learning bias of this activity is towards music listening leading to an understanding of phrasing. At another time the bias might lean towards dancing and much more attention will be given to acquiring the moves and formations of a jig.

Standing, fairly well spaced out, in a circle.

Phrase 1 – Tap knees for 8 beats, clap hands quietly for 8. Repeat.
Phrase 2 – Step forward for 8 beats, step back for 8. Repeat.
Phrase 3 – Hold hands and circle to the right for 16 steps.
Phrase 4 – Circle to the left for 16 steps.

The 6/8 meter of the jig gives a feel of 2 beats to a bar, making 8 bars to each phrase.

∿ The complete 32 bar jig is repeated two more times.

The second jig begins now and has the same four phrase, thirty two bar structure but is only played twice and not three times as in the first jig. The children could sit and tap knees, clap hands quietly for eight counts throughout the jig and listen carefully for the way in which the melody is decorated with small trills and extra decorative notes.

The pattern of phrases in Tommy Peoples' 'Two Jigs' is typical of traditional dance form and will be found over and over again in all kinds of dances. To couple two dances together without a break is also usual; sometimes several tunes are chained in this way.

Whether children are able to listen for and sense musically the phrasing and form of the music when they investigate, compose or perform. Some children may rely on counting out the phrasing – can they move on from using counting as a support to using the musical cues given in melody, harmony, rhythm, tempo to indicate the phrasing structure of individual pieces of music?

Simple movement patterning as a strategy for exploring phrase structure, as suggested in this activity, can easily be applied to any British folk dance form. Once children have had experience of dancing jigs and an understanding of how the musical form and the dance form work hand in hand, they can begin to compose their own dances (see: Upton and Paine, 1996).

performance style

The basic single line melodies and rhythm patterns of Irish traditional music are relatively simple: the musical 'bare bones'. These melodies are usually handed on aurally from player to player in informal play together sessions. Each performer is then expected to give their own creative stamp to the music by improvising decorations of the basic melody. The player will add quick, extra notes, ornaments and slides between notes to embroider the original tune. Listening carefully again to Tommy Peoples children will be able to hear all the small decorative additions he plays.

Here is a jig to perform:

This jig could be sung or would sound good played as a solo on whistle, recorder, or violin. Notice the phrases which repeat exactly the same or with slight differences at the end and those which are new. And be sure to repeat the phrases as marked. Once known, each child can begin to work on finding ways to ornament their playing. If there are notes out of the players' range, perhaps in the fourth phrase, the children can simply make their own alternative versions to play. Two or more players can go on to play the melody together in unison for others to dance to.

individual progression

The seven year old transferring from early primary to later primary schooling will hopefully have had experience of and be able to keep movements in time with music of medium pace. If given practice in the early years, children should be competent at adjusting their movement tempo to keep in time with others. They can be expected to have a vocabulary of whole body movements drawn from prior dance, PE and play experiences which will enable them to respond with increasing imagination in dance listening and choreographing activities.

As the child progresses through the later primary years, they will gain greater movement control and coordination and awareness of how to coordinate their dancing with the music. As a result of this experience, they will be able to move in time with music heard and maintain a steady tempo in their own music-making at faster and slower paces and to coordinate more complex rhythm patterns. From these experiences they will build a conceptual understanding of rhythm and time structures which is rooted in physical experience of dancing. They will become physically stronger and able to find more variety and quality of movement. They gain in the ability to organise, alter and develop their movements into dances sequences and can compose longer stretches of dance and movement work.

music, words and drama

Music linked with words and story-telling, drama, ritual or theatre, has cultural roots as deep as those of music and dance. Children find music theatre of all kinds exciting and compelling, whether as participants or audience. There are endless possibilities for exploration of different forms in which music, words and drama are brought together. This can include:

● setting words to music with a feel for characterisation, mood and expression;
● using voices dramatically across the spectrum from speech to rap to chant to song;

- setting words side by side with music to complement each other;
- making music for different kinds of story telling and music drama.

planning points

The first set of activities suggested here work well for individuals or pairs. They grow out of language work and can be offered as occasional opportunities alongside other creative writing activities. Whole class time can be used to investigate the possibilities and to introduce and practise related skills, with a few children taking up the ideas and bringing their work back later for discussion. There is no need for every child to try out the ideas all at the same time, or even in the same term. Once children have experience of using words and music together in these ways, they find their own opportunities for music in the context of writing or drama. The aim is that these possibilities become part of each child's repertoire of creative skills and forms; for some children they may take on a more significant role.

The second set of ideas is more drama-based and is most likely to arise within the context of a class project with a range of opportunities for individual or group composing and performing. Organisationally, this work may need to be strongly teacher-led but it is crucial that the children have plenty of scope for their own composition and also for contributing to performance decisions.

spoken words and music

Linking music with language work, there is a great deal of scope, in addition to song-writing, for creative writing and musical composition to be evolved side by side in a number of formats based on spoken word or chant and music. Possibilities include rap, which is essentially an improvised performance genre but can easily lend itself to composed material too, other forms of chant or speech-rhythm based music, music composed to precede or follow poetry read aloud, and spoken word combined with live or electro-acoustic music. These forms can work as free-standing presentations or in the context of drama.

The music-language connection helps children's creative

development in both areas. Using words in a musical context encourages children to be aware of the sound of language and of word rhythm, speech intonation and expression, and to take this into account in their writing and speaking as well as in musical composition or performance. Putting words into a performance context helps children build confidence in communicating with words. Composing music to go with words encourages deeper engagement with the meaning of text and with ways of interpreting text creatively. This also enhances sensitivity to text meaning in performance. Whether in singing or in speech, the skills of clear diction, control of breathing and dynamics, and making sense of phrase shape can all be developed.

rap

Rap is for communicating ideas, individual viewpoints, commentary, and for eliciting action or reaction. It works well as a format for creative speaking or writing about an issue of any kind e.g. an environmental or social issue. It can also work as a form within a drama as a vehicle for certain characters to give their viewpoint e.g. one of Columbus's sailors, thirty days out to sea.

Listen to some examples of rap, as recent as can be found – children may have examples of their own. This is indispensable, since above all successful rapping depends on picking up the performance style itself. The best strategy is for children to make their own guidelines for composing a rap by listing stylistic features of the examples they've listened to.

Some preliminary classwork on diction and rhythm skills will help. This might include:

activities

~ make chants over a rhythmic beat (played on knee, foot-tapping, shaker) out of any words, *e.g. nonsense, or rhyming words*; concentrate on sequencing words so that the word rhythms fit in with the beat; explore voice characteristics *e.g. tone and expression of voice, varying pitch and dynamics as you try the chants out*;

~ listen to electronic backing beats *e.g. a pre-programmed beat selected from a keyboard (tape recorded if necessary) or a pattern programmed into a drum machine or computer*; clap, tap, move, dance to the beat; discuss and get the feel of the completely regular, unvarying quality of an automated beat; if you prefer, go on to make your own backing to get the effect you want;

- practise performing any chant (as above) against a pre-set electronic backing bcat; try different speeds and discover what works well;
- if working in groups, try some different groupings *e.g. solo and chorus, one line each round different voices, alternating solo with short interjections for two or more, two groups alternating antiphonally.*

Write, rehearse, perform and record a rap of your own.

Take time to think about what you want to communicate and to choose language that works well.

Consider each skill aspect above. Listen to drafts of your work i.e. don't just read it silently.

Perform live to an audience, with staged movements/dance as appropriate.

music with words

Music and words do not do the same things. They cannot replace each other. They cannot communicate in the same way. Music is not a language. Music and words can complement each other. Each can also provide a stimulus for creative response in the other medium. Words can suggest music; music can suggest words.

For some children, a very fruitful way to work is to compose words for music, music for words, or words and music, where in each case the intention is that they be heard side by side. This is not song-writing or background music; it is work in two media, exploring an idea across both. As in rap, it requires hearing words as sound as well as meaning.

music with haiku

activity

- Choose or write a haiku. Any short poem would work; haiku have the particular power of their distinctive syllable patterns and of crystallising images or sense in a very compact way. Read it aloud, think about and internalise the imaginative impact of the text. Compose music to be performed after the poem has been read. The time span can be viewed in two ways:
  - make music to match almost exactly the length of the poem *or*
  - make music which expands on the experience of the poem, as it were unpacking it or taking it on somewhere else.

- Try listening to the poem and then listen for imagined music in your head; what does it sound like? *even if it's hard to do, this stresses the aspect of hearing the two side by side; it encourages composing which works from aural imagery 'outwards' rather than from hardware to sound.*
- Choose a single instrument or voice; make one short motif or idea which might capture the feel of the words; try several of these; discuss how the music might be developed from the motif; try turning the idea into a piece.

words and technology

Practical activities need to be supported by listening to music by composers who have incorporated the spoken word into their music. The following is an example of this; in this case the composer has used technology to bring recorded speech, and also train sounds, into music performed by a string quartet as well.

Steve Reich: *Different Trains*

Different Trains (1988) is a piece in three sections, each based on a different train: *America – Before the war*, *Europe – During the war* and *After the war*. The music played by the four string instruments is derived from pitches generated by the recorded speech and train sounds. The speech patterns suggest both rhythmic and pitch motifs which are repeated and transformed. This is an idea Reich had explored in earlier taped pieces such as *It's Gonna Rain* and it is one which children can try out for themselves in either taped or live versions.

America – Before the war uses similar layering, phasing, and shifting techniques found in Reich's 'abstract' music. Here though, the sound images tie up with the perpetual motion of the train, and the two-tone, then one-tone whistle. Changes of speed also have both musical and representational function. Reich writes:

'the piece presents both a documentary and a musical reality, and begins a new musical direction. It is a direction that I expect will lead to a new kind of documentary music video theatre in the not too distant future.'

Children can discuss this as an idea for a function of music and one which they can incorporate into history work for themselves.

Think about the skills the players need to perform this piece:
- managing to do the same thing over and over again;
- keeping steady beats, steady enough to sound mechanical;
- keeping together;
- knowing where you are, how many times to play each bit, perhaps fitting in with a tape;
- recording your bit, possibly without knowing what the whole piece will sound like.

These descriptions are from Year 5 and 6 children listening to this music as part of their own composing work:

> *'I think that the tune is good because it sounded like a train and it was fast and rushy.'*

> *'it's going to burst out, like the River Dance'*

> *'he composed his tune by getting people to do speeches and then put rhythms to them'*

> *'it has little speeches between the tune, and the rhythm changes to the voice change and speech change'*

> *'it changes tempo with different speeches then slows at the end to signal that the piece is finishing'*

> *'The tune I liked because it was different from any of the tunes I have ever heard. I also liked it because it made me think lots of different things.'*

> *'It was probably good because it had some modern technology and many classics didn't have that.'*

> *'I like this piece of music because he has thought about it very hard. It took him ages to get it organised and I like it.'*

The children enjoyed this music but much more than that, it interested them. Listening alongside their own composing activities they realised something of the complexity of the processes that went into putting this together.

activity

➤ Use any combination of music and speech, either live with voice and microphone or pre-recorded tape and recorded or live music, to present documentary ideas; this might be reporting a news story, being an eye-witness to an historic event, or showing an aspect of ordinary life.

music and drama

There are numerous occasions in school when drama becomes an exciting and useful vehicle for exploring a topic, bringing history to life, or becoming immersed in story. More formally, assembly often calls for dramatised presentations. Or there may be a custom of presenting dramatic performances to parents, perhaps at festive seasons or as an end of term venture. Children's learning from such projects can be cross-curricular. In any such project children should be producing quality creative work of their own and have some real ownership of the processes of composing, rehearsing and performance decision-making. Much of this is lost if they are merely passive participants being told what to say, do, sing and play. The latter situation can arise if what is attempted is too big or ambitious in scope; the best learning often occurs from smaller scale work in which children have been able to take a full part.

Music composed for story or drama in school can be very low level, amounting to little more than sound effects. One cause of this is a lack of experience of listening to music conceived for theatre of different kinds. Without detailed thought and discussion about how music can be constructed to have the required dramatic impact, children fall back on a handful of stereotypes or a sequence of effects which do not hang together as music at all. Hearing and seeing the work of other composers on video, or best of all live, is the only way to gain a wider understanding of how music can function dramatically and yet still make sense in its own right. The following sections are intended to suggest approaches to particular aspects of the task of matching music with drama. Many are based on borrowing other composer's ideas, often the best source of new inspiration.

making dramatic music from a story

Very often the starting point for creating a piece of music theatre is a story which already has its own shape, characters and setting. Before attempting to create music which will dramatise the story children need to be very familiar with the story itself and have discussed in general its dramatic possibilities.

The first decisions to be made relate to exactly what you want the music to do. It might:
● set the scenes and atmosphere;
● accompany dance or mime;
● be used to tell the whole story, with characters singing some or all of the time;
● be used between scenes of a play;
● add sound effects.

For the music to work well, it must:
● add an extra dimension to the drama, not distract attention from it;
● make sense as music in its own right.

A good way to start is to break the story down into stages; a 'storyboard' format can be used for this. Think about each section in terms of its dramatic events, character, and mood. Then consider if and how music might contribute to each bit. It might be clear that instrumental music would fit in one place, a song or dance in another, and so on. Key questions are:
● what is the dramatic point here? the feeling? the impact? the situation?
● what exactly will the music's function here be? what will the audience experience?
● what *musical* techniques will give the required effect? how will it hold together as *music*?

Making the translation from dramatic idea into musical form is the difficult bit. So often story music founders because it is no more than sound effects. It is essential to try to find musical forms to match the dramatic needs of the moment. This might be done by:
● mapping out the dramatic structure of the scene in terms of mood and pace, then using this outline as a framework for composing music to match;

- finding a musical pattern or idea which captures one aspect of the moment or of a character, then building music from this 'motif'; think about rhythm, pitch and timbre;
- analysing a character's thoughts, feelings and intentions, and using music to portray these in a song; think about speed, rhythm, melodic character, and voice quality.

It will be necessary to try things out, listen carefully and adapt accordingly. Listen to the music on its own. Does it make sense as music? This is the crucial test.

The following investigations look at some different musical formats encountered in music dramas and link practical ideas to examples from different kinds of music theatre pieces.

characters through music

If solo characters in a drama are to sing their own songs, or to have a theme associated with them, some thought can be given to how the music can work to best effect.

In Judith Weir's ten minute opera *King Harald* for solo soprano, the single voice is used to take the characters of King Harald, his dead brother Olaf, the evil Tostig, a boy messenger, King Harald's two wives and the whole Norwegian army. Yet each of these is vividly portrayed. Techniques used include:
- using rhythm patterning to convey aggression, calm, authority, reminiscing;
- using the sound of words to support character – hard or soft consonants etc.;
- using voice quality and pitch range to support character;
- using dynamic variety in different ways – contrasts, levels, accent.

Meredith Monk's piece *The Tale* (from *The Education of The Girl Child*) is written for voice and piano; on the KOCH International Classics CD this is performed by a male pianist who uses his own voice to portray an old woman. This vocal timbre, as well as the way the voice is used, gives an immediately vivid picture of the speaker. First the piano is heard playing pattern based music and generating quite a rhythmic feel; we could hear it as crotchety or impatient but also vigorous. Next are heard voice sounds, no words, but laughter, 'ha ha ha, mm mm, ho ho he he'; then words, spoken, a kind of intoning, very stretched out.

I still have my hands
I still have my memory
I still have my gold ring
beautiful I love it I love it
I still have my allergies
I still have my philosophies

It is very strong theatre, out of very simple means, and is a good example of creating character through different ways of using the voice.

In Britten's *Noye's Fludde* the animals in procession are characterised by higher voices the smaller they are. In *A Midsummer Night's Dream* all the voices of the supernatural fairy characters are in some way unusual in operatic terms – boys, a counter-tenor, a coloratura soprano, and Puck speaks, always accompanied by a snare drum. Hildegard, in *Ordo Virtutum* (*The Play of the Virtues*), one of the oldest musical plays, gives each character – Obedience, Hope, etc. – a characteristic voice range and mode or set of notes; she gives the Devil a speaking-only part, since he is too evil to have music. When making music for a character, think about:

● the quality and pitch of voice;
● how they move, walk, stride: use this to help find rhythm patterns which give character; try pairing up a mover/dancer with a vocalist or instrumentalist who mirrors their actions – listening carefully;
● their state of mind: calm, angry, tense, afraid.. how might this be portrayed in sound?

These questions can also be used when discussing music listened to; this is the best way to gather up ideas.

activity

~ Write a short scene for a character alone on stage, introducing themselves or reminiscing about some past deed or event. Set it to music, using some of the ideas above.

scene setting

The key here is again not to settle for sound effects, even if these play some part. The music must work in its own right. Check this by considering whether an audience could listen to the music without the drama or story and still make sense of it. Think about this at two levels. At the larger scale, the music must have some coherent shape. For example, it might gradually build and thicken and get louder; or there may be a constant backwash of a particular instrumental colour or rhythmic figure while lots of small sounds and effects take place over the top.

Listen to, for example:

- the opening of Britten's *A Midsummer Night's Dream*: deep instruments slide up and down...;
- Adams' 'The Landing of the Spirit of '76' in *Nixon in China*: opens with a gradual build-up culminating on a single chord which then alternates rhythmically with another;
- music for gamelan associated with a telling with shadow puppets of the Ramayana: players in front of the screen follow the action musically by varying speed and dynamics.

These pieces all show how a composer can use the musical elements of rhythm, melody, timbre and dynamics to turn sound effects into music whilst still creating an appropriate atmosphere. This can only be judged by trying ideas out and listening. This can be practised in reverse, starting with a musical feature and listening to what it suggests. For example:

activities

- Sets of notes: Commission groups to work on particular scales: e.g. C D E F sharp G sharp A sharp; discuss the music which results in relation to the character given by the note set.
- Ostinato: Make ostinati (repeating patterns) which use different tempi, rhythm and pitch patterns, and which use one timbre or combine two or three. Collect these on tape. Listen and discuss the mood each sets and why.
- Dynamics and tempo: In a small group of players, follow the lead of a drummer in varying speed and dynamics as in Balinese gamelan. Listen to the dramatic effects which result and discuss.

Dialogue, action and interaction

●————————————————————————————————————

Stephen Sondheim *Sunday in the Park with George*

Another form of scene setting which runs into dialogue, using speech and music together, can be heard in the opening of Sondheim's *Sunday in the Park with George*. The show is based on the painting by George Seurat 1859-91 *A Sunday Afternoon on the Island of La Grande Jatte* (in The Art Institute of Chicago) of Parisien promenaders enjoying a summer Sunday's leisure in a park along the Seine. The first sound – a spread chord on the piano – seems to relate to the style of the painting – Divisionism, Pointillism. Each of the opening words of the painter: 'Design. Tension. Composition. Balance. Light. Harmony.' are punctuated by piano and percussion, using bells and very light timbres. This transforms, as does the scene into a duet, spoken at first between George Seurat and his model, Dot. She speaks, over a piano 'um pah' at first: 'George. Why is it you always get to sit in the shade while I have to stand in the sun? Hello George. There is someone in this dress.' As she gets increasingly impatient, trying to catch the painter's attention, the speech becomes patterned rhythmically first, and then pitched: 'Sunday in the park with George' – a melodic motif which later builds into a whole number. The audience are drawn into the action and music in a way which exactly parallels moving from the real world into a picture. The end of the whole show reverses the process.

————————————————————————————————————●

Musical duets allow actors to sing in turn or to sing at the same time, either combining their efforts harmoniously or putting their own point of view in music supports conflict and animosity or humour. Papageno and Papagena's duet from Mozart's *Magic Flute* is an example which shows how this can happen in a very strictly contained musical form.

| activity |

⤳ Write a short conversation between two characters in a story and set it to music for unaccompanied voices, using the above ideas; e.g. Max and his mother in Sendak's *Where The Wild Things Are*.

Choruses

Chorus items can be very effective using quite simple means as long as they are easy enough to be performed reliably and with confidence. The musical structures need to match the occasion. The '*Morning of the Dragon*' chorus from Schonberg's *Miss Saigon*, with chorus first in unison over a drum beat and later adding a second part, but still with a very sparse texture has a forceful and dramatic effect matched by marching feet. 'The people are the heroes now..' from Adams' *Nixon in China* uses chanting in unison, built on very simple phrases, but with varied and compelling rhythms, often syncopated, and alternating smoother held notes with short clipped chanting.

<table>
<tr><td>

activity

</td><td>

~ With the whole class, try improvising small sections of chorus music using any of the following structures:
- everyone keeping together obviously gives a sense of unity;
- two opposing factions can be set in opposition by using a turn taking structure across physical space, antiphonally;
- a round with each part entering at different times can give an impression of a crowd talking amongst themselves;
- a solo interrupted by short interjections from the chorus can give a heightened sense of drama;
- a small group singing with a larger group humming behind can give a calm or solemn feel.

Different tones of voice and whispering, chanting, speaking, singing and shouting can all be used to increase the impact. To begin with use pitch patterns with very few notes, one note, or even random notes while the effect in general is tried out.
~ Ask a listening group to comment on the effect overall, or record, listen and discuss.

</td></tr>
</table>

individual progression

Building on early years' experience of working with language and drama, children in this age-phase develop a growing awareness of the potential of bringing these areas together with music. Individuals will have their own creative responses to the potential offered by these media and can be given the scope to pursue particular interests. The development of skills of handling words and music together depends on the child's understanding of both language and musical elements. Some children have a much greater sense of drama than others, but this can to some extent be 'caught' and built on.

More widely, once children's attention is drawn to the elements of dance, music and language work and how these interrelate, they will increasingly be able to make informed decisions and judgments about their own work. Confidence will develop in relation to the degree of freedom and independence children are given to incorporate their own ideas and imagination into their work.

assessment points

early stages

The child:
- can dance with music keeping to the beat using simple travelling steps at a moderate speed;
- knows some different styles of dancing and dance music and can talk about dance music using simple terms;
- shows, through composing, listening and performing, a developing sense of the power of bringing music together with words and drama.

later stages

The child:
- can dance in time with music using a variety of movements and across a wide range of speeds;
- knows a number of different dances from other times and places; can talk about dance music using musical terms to describe the musical elements of duration, metre, tempo and form;
- has developed a range of understanding and skills in using music in relation to words and drama.

music tools

primary music: later years

A whole class music lesson carried out with just the teacher's voice, a piano and an overhead of song words is a useful way to engage children in certain kinds of spontaneous activity – a rote-learnt song, a skill game, an improvised movement to music session. But these teaching approaches, supported by the equipment that are part of them, while doing some things, restrict others. To broaden and deepen children's learning, music teaching needs to be delivered through a wide range of teaching formats (see earlier section on 'maximising opportunities') and to make use of other teaching strategies. Integral to these teaching approaches are ways of encouraging children to engage in the musical processes from which musical understanding will develop. Tools, as they have been termed in this section, are just that, the means which enable the child to become deeply involved in the workings of music. Three 'tools' have been identified:

- notations;
- technologies;
- notebooks.

Each in turn becomes the focus for the following sections.

notations

The class (Y5) have listened seven times already to the one-minute opening section of a piece recorded by the Steve Miller Band long ago. Each child is working with coloured pens on a large piece of paper on the table in front of them. This is not art work, not making a picture in response to the music, though it might have been. The task is to draw the music, to map it out on the paper, showing 'how it goes'. Strangely enough, as the repeats have gone on interest has grown. The announcement that this is the last hearing is met with groans from more than a few. It's as if each hearing is bringing to light yet another layer of the music, or another aspect of detail, missed before.

The music is electronic, with an introduction in which a series of different sound events are sequenced over a dark and insistent drone. At the point at which the music is faded out, these effects melt

Into a regular, jazzy kind of backing beat with a melodic pattern overlaid.

In the discussion about the music which follows, an extraordinary range of perceptions emerge; children pick out different aspects in different ways, and the scores are a prompt to remembering and conceptualising the musical structures. The different ways in which they have made relationships between sound and symbol in their drawings contribute to this, detailing particular musical elements and showing development over time. This medium has clearly also incorporated a subjective element into the representations: one child insists that the drone 'sounds thick and black', another that 'the sparkly bits are bright like stars'.

A music notation can be, as in this example, a piece of analysis, a thinking tool, a map. It can also be a way of encoding information in order to pass it from composer or arranger to performer, or a way of recording and storing musical sound for reference or retrieval by scholars or for posterity. The many ways in which different musics can be notated are to differing degrees efficient in relation to their particular functions. All, however, become meaningful only within an understood practice which somehow establishes the relation between sound and symbol. This may be a temporary practice invented today by me for my own use; or it may be a widely understood set of conventions such as those governing standard staff notation.

For most children, the ability to use notations in any of the above ways increases rapidly from the age of seven or thereabouts alongside the development in their abilities to grasp in more abstract forms the musical ideas which are founded on structures in time and on mathematical patternings – of number, measure, sequence and shape. As their understanding of representation of all kinds develops, the scope also widens for representing the more physical, surface aspects of musical timbre and texture.

mapping music

In the example above, notation is being used as a tool to deepen a certain kind of analytical listening, whilst leaving some scope for responsive interpretation too, since children are not restricted to any particular parameters e.g. of duration or pitch and can choose how to portray any aspect in the way they 'see' it. The task allows for differentiation as each child works within their own capabilities and understanding. The teacher can work with two processes here:

● the aural analysis involved in translating sound into visual structures; *'writing'*;
● reflection on the music after hearing: having the score to refer to facilitates this; *'reading'*.

The former is a process of picking out and conceptualising the constituent parts of the music and the temporal and other relationships between them. The latter is a process of considering how the separate aspects relate, and bringing together the musical experience with the understanding of how the music is made up. Broadly they can be conceived of as 'writing' and 'reading', where each entails bringing a wider awareness to the translation. Together these contribute to:

● a greater listening awareness of this and other music;
● a greater understanding of how composers structure their music and a widening fund of ideas to draw on in composing;
● a more acute sense of how performers shape musical sound as they produce it.

Mapping activities are best used intensely but occasionally, aiming for maximum involvement and attention to detail. Teachers can focus discussion afterwards in any of the above directions. If children have become really immersed in the activity, the quality of talk which follows can be very high indeed. Individuals can use listening and scoring of this kind to investigate music of their own choice, working with headphones and a listening centre and making notes of their own thoughts afterwards. For younger children or less experienced children, some preparatory activities in mapping short sequences, perhaps played live by the teacher and using classroom instruments, can help to stage the work.

communicating music

Perhaps the most familiar uses of music notations are those by which a composer communicates to unseen and unknown performers what to do and how, in order to 'realise' (literally) a piece of her or his music. The demand for this kind of notation to be free-standing and independent of the composer's presence as an interpreter is relatively recent in historical terms. Goehr points out that: 'Only at the end of the eighteenth century did individual instrumental compositions begin to be thought about as self-sufficient works, each publishable in its own right' (Goehr, 1992). Furthermore, until this time, composers usually directed performances of their own music, or performed it themselves, and the distinction of the two roles was much less significant.

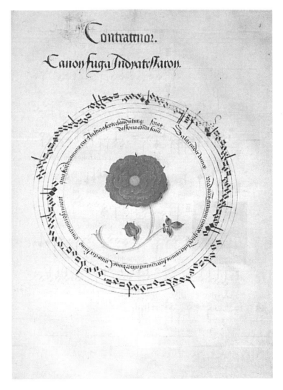

Royal MS 11 E.XI, ff 2V, 3, Canon in honour of Henry VIII, Salve radix. Reproduced by permission of The British Library. The music is for four voices, two bass (on the left hand side) and two countertenor (on the right).

The two main types of notation currently used for communication between composers or arrangers and performers are:
- staff notation;
- graphic notation.

These record musical data in different ways and the different bases they use in conveying what is required determines which is appropriate for the music in question. Occasionally they are used by composers in combination so as to cover a wider spectrum of information. In educational contexts, graphic notation is sometimes seen as an easy way of introducing notational concepts. It would be a misconception in terms of wider musical practice, however, to see graphic notation as a less precise way of writing music. Both systems have precision of different kinds and each has areas of vagueness. It is important to keep sight of this when working with children and to be clear about the specific functions of any form of notation in use.

children using notation

For children in the 7–11 range, genuine purposes for using either of the above systems for communication is limited. This does not invalidate introducing notation as a tool and developing literacy skills in respect of both staff and graphic notational forms. On the contrary, this age-phase is an excellent time to do this, since children are often well motivated towards gaining understanding which represents a passport into another aspect of adult knowledge. But it is important for teachers to be honest about the purposes of learning activities in this field.

As composers, the ability of most children in this age-phase to make music far outstrips their ability to notate it in any form. Their memories are such that they usually do not need a notation to remind them how the piece goes. As part of the working process, a tape recorder provides a much quicker and more effective prompt if any is needed. And, like composers of earlier periods or musicians within aural traditions, they are in close contact with their performers or they perform their work themselves.

As performers, children mostly embark on learning to read notation alongside learning an instrument. The notational system used, and the order in which its elements are introduced depends on the instrument and the style of music. For example:

- recorder players learn staff notation on a single stave with a treble clef 𝄞, beginning with a few notes, often G A B, which are easiest to play. Tunes are often restricted early on to simple rhythms, not for musical reasons but to make reading easier;
- pianists learn staff notation but this may begin with two thumbs on middle C, playing the same note, yet each notated on a separate stave, one with treble clef and one with bass clef 𝄢;
- trombonists read from staff notation, but learn with a treble clef if they play in a brass band or a bass clef if they play in an orchestra;
- folk guitar players learn a notation based on chord letter names; classical guitarists learn from a single stave, which requires many leger (additional) lines above and below; they may also use tablature notations, deriving from early lute music, in which guitar strings are represented semi-graphically.

Whichever system is used, learning to read from music as a performer in 'real time', that is, at the speed at which the music goes, is a long process. Most 7–8 year olds, even if they are learning an instrument are in the early stages of this. There will be times when it is useful, therefore, not to tie musical performance too tightly to what children can read. Learning aurally and by memory, and playing improvised music redresses the balance between eye and ear. In the case of singing, children can sing from music which uses notation, but they will rely on ear and memory for detail of pitch and rhythm. Again, the process of learning to perform from notated music as a singer is a long one, with greater demands on the ear and understanding in order to pitch accurately.

Honesty therefore entails being straightforward with children about the uses of notation, and staging learning so that they can acquire literacy effectively and gradually, without this hindering progress in other musical skills. There need be no pressure about this, and how far to go in introducing staff notation will be a matter for each school to decide. Skills of notating and of reading notations continue to develop through secondary education and into adult life for those who have uses for them. As a general approach, during the later primary years teaching can support:

- a broad understanding for all children of the range of notations and purposes for them;
- basic skill development in using notations across the range of musical elements, e.g. ways of recording and reading timbre, pitch, rhythm, harmony, texture and dynamics, though not necessarily in combination;
- extended development of particular notation skills in relation to the needs determined by individual music pathways – as composers, singers and instrumentalists.

As with language literacy, if it is to make sense, learning to read and write music must trail behind the ability to 'use' music in practice.

staff notation

Conventional staff notation conveys relatively specific information about musical pitch and rhythm. It also gives an analogue of sounds occurring in time, spatially represented on a page as moving from left to right. By aligning different layers of the music it is also indicates which sounds are heard at the same time. It gives a pictorial representation of pitch as 'higher' or 'lower' on a page so that melodic contours look like line shapes in space.

At the beginning of the 7–11 age-range, children may have little experience of using staff notation or they may have been introduced to the beginnings of pitch or rhythm notation, taken separately. It is usually wise to continue to use simplified notations of rhythm and pitch separately for the first year or so, as well as introducing examples of complete staff notation for children to see. The aim will be to let a broad understanding of notations soak in as part of the whole range of musical contexts in which they might be used.

rhythm

Sets of rhythm cards, each containing a simple notated pattern are often used for 'look and play' or 'look and sing' skill practice. At the simplest level, cards might show:

Later, patterns may be represented as:

It requires some thought, however, to how such activities can be given a musical context. For example,

activities

~ Perform patterns individually; play it, think it, play it; discuss how each differs in character; consider what it is about the arrangement of notes which gives a particular effect.

~ Use a limited number of cards (3–6, not always 4); having tried them out individually as above, one child arranges them in sequence. All perform the sequence and discuss as above.

~ As above, choose a sequence. Before performing it, discuss how it will sound. Then try it and listen.

~ Try and compare different sequences; ask everyone to choose one they enjoy and perform this together.

~ Take one or more sequences and explore different dynamics in performing it. Include accents and play with moving these around.

~ Use single patterns as accompaniments to songs, or as starting ideas for instrumental pieces.

~ Later, reverse the process and work out notations for rhythm patterns which arise in songs or instrumental pieces.

Activities such as these can be returned to for short sessions, occasionally or frequently, and adapted and elaborated on by children as well as teachers. Best results follow as patterns become well-known; staying with a small set until children know them inside out gives a level of control and accuracy which leads to much more musical results.

Pattern sets should be based on different metres, i.e. grouped in 3, 4 or 5 beats. Children move quite easily between these and an extension for older children is to make sequences using both three and four beat groupings mixed.

<table>
<tr><td>notice</td><td>

- the quality of listening to the effect of each pattern;
- whether children are reading, memorising or listening only;
- children's ability to perform patterns in 'real' time, keeping up.

</td></tr>
</table>

melody

Melodic notation, on the other hand, is better approached in the context of melody writing. A simplified system of using notes without rhythm values makes an easy beginning. Children can work first with just outline shapes:

and later with notes on a stave.

In some programmes, computer notations use this same kind of progression from a simplified notation towards a conventional staff notation. In the example below, the five lines with an additional sixth line below correspond to a stave; notes are placed with the mouse and played back to the composer. The grid represents even divisions of time. Children may approach the composing task visually initially, but soon begin to work with sound and to tie the two aspects together. Debbie (Year 4) commented, 'First I did straight lines but thought *"boring"* so I took every second one out and placed it higher. Straight lines sounded boring so I moved the second ones up.'

graphic notation

Graphic notations are much less standardised than staff notation and are used when a composer wants to convey different kinds of information to performers. They are often very specific about time lengths, measured off in minutes or seconds, within which certain musical events are placed. Graphic scores usually incorporate a wide range of markings, from shapes, lines and squiggles to words and phonics, and often include passages in staff notation as well. It is by no means always correct to assume that a graphic score is vaguer. It may be very precise over instructions to performers and cover the notation of elements such as timbre and dynamics with a precision for which staff notation has no equivalent.

Graphic notations are sometimes used in situations where the composer wants to allow the performer more freedom, either for structured improvisation, or to interpret a symbol in whatever way he or she chooses. In this case, the notation is playing a different kind of communicative role, and the performer may be given control over more elements of the ultimate musical sound than conventional notations usually allow. Graphic notations may use space on a page moving from left to right to represent time or take another pathway. Some music requires that certain music is played but leaves the sequencing up to the performer. The page may lay out material through which the performer chooses their own route.

Children may have early experience of drawing symbols to stand for musical sound or patterns in the way that they might be represented on a graphic score. In the school context, however, there is sometimes confusion about how graphic scores are being used. Inventing symbols may be seen as a stage on the way to learning staff notation; in this case, the purpose is to establish the idea of symbols representing sound before specific conventions are introduced. Essentially though, graphic scores introduce a different range of functions and through the later primary years children can be expected to think about the ways scores hold information and to choose to use whatever scoring is most appropriate to the task in hand.

Graphic scores may be used to record the instrumental layers in a composition, giving a rough indication of stops, starts and timbre, as in this example:

Or they can give additional information, for instance, about pitch and dynamics, as here:

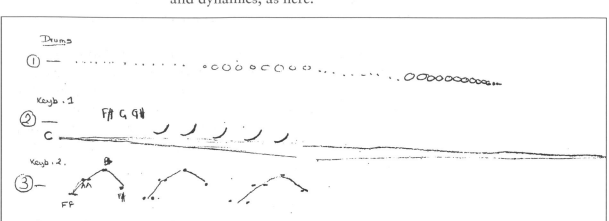

Some computer software offers graphic score tools, more like a drawing programme which are then played back with the composer's choice of timbres. Pitch can be controlled precisely if enough trouble is taken and time is tracked by a moving line, rather than in measured beats.

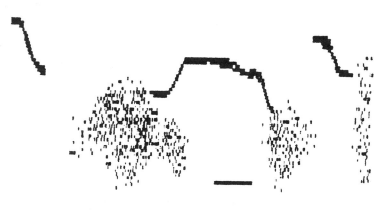

The following activities indicate some examples of how children's understanding of graphic scores can be built on from these beginnings as they move through the age-range.

activities

~ Draw a time line or grid with time measured into equal spaces. Use a watch to count seconds and to decide how long each measure will be. Experiment with one or two players improvising while listeners show the music by using counters, multilink, stones, shells or string placed along the time line. Vary the music and the notation and listen to the changes. Focus on developing an accurate sense of time measured in seconds.

- Work with two players on scoring the relationship between two separate lines of music. Start with continuous parallel lines, one for each to play as unbroken music. Move a pointer along above the lines at a steady speed; players stop at the end of their line. Experiment with removing parts of one or both lines, so that players stop and start together or at different times. Focus on exploring the possibilities for different textures.

- Make and score some music for voice or one instrument that uses different timbres. Devise ways of showing these differences as accurately as possible by drawing symbols for the sound. It may be possible to incorporate scoring the dynamics too. Focus on the use of drawing techniques to convey timbre and dynamics precisely.

Work on notation cannot be separated from musical sound and understanding. If manipulating notation is allowed to become the foreground objective, musical sense can be easily lost. Using notations as tools which allow children to reach a deeper and more alert understanding of musical structures and possibilities can be extremely effective. Allowing what is suggested by the relationships between the aural and the visual to interact can be exciting territory for musical exploration.

music technologies

In striking contrast to rapid and far-reaching technological developments in the music world at large, primary music remains surprisingly 'low-tech'. Some music technology may have crept into the primary classroom, the computer set up with music software and a CD ROM of musical information, there may be a keyboard with headphones, but in general these inroads into technology remain on the fringes and are not integrated into mainstream primary music teaching. Beyond the primary school, at home, in the community and later in the secondary schools they will transfer to, children are likely to come into close contact with music and musical activities which incorporate technology in some way. Increasingly, outside school, children have access to computers, karaoke sets, CD players and video, keyboards, multimedia workstations which enable them to acquire self-taught proficiencies. If primary schools are to connect up with the wider culture of music beyond the primary school, technologies will play an increasingly important role in primary school music.

There are many reasons which are common to primary ICT education in general to explain why music technologies are not widely filtering into music education; the high costs of equipment, unfamiliarity on the part of teachers, 'technophobia' even, belief that technology will not add to what is already being achieved and so on. Without wishing to diminish the impact of these factors, when equipment is seriously believed in, barriers are usually overcome. Beneath these surface practicalities lie reasons embedded in the practice of primary music itself. The new technologies change children's relationship with music and restructure the way in which they learn. This challenges and destabilises established ways of teaching and learning. Imagine what children's technology assisted music-making might look and sound like:

- Two children have fixed a pick-up to a xylophone to play it through an amplifier and have added reverb effects. With this sound they are playing a bass riff to a song they are learning to sing. They will record the bass part and then play it karaoke style to accompany their own singing.
- A recorder player has recorded short snatches of melody and fed them into a sequencer which can loop the short melodic ideas. He will add another layer of sequenced melodic ideas and build up a composition in this way.
- Two children are interested in learning percussion skills; the teacher suggests they research on the Internet. They have to decide on a key word to search on (similar to library search procedures) and then visit various sites, printing off some information they think will be valuable. They e-mail the percussionist Evelyn Glennie from her web site.
- A performance is being prepared for assembly for which one child will sing a pop song using a microphone and amplifier to enlarge the sound and slightly alter the timbre of his voice. He is accompanied by keyboard. Two girls are setting up the

equipment in the hall and listening carefully for balance levels between the keyboard and singer, making adjustments to the equipment as necessary.

- Two children are practising an aural listening game at the computer. When complete, they fetch the discs on which they are keeping a log of all their musical activity. They load up and under one file make a note of this practice session.

This set of pictures of music technology in practice represents a complex set of approaches which will blend with, extend and enhance children's music learning in many areas. Ideally music technology is not seen as a separate area which is tacked on to what is already in place but is seen as an exciting and important development to the way in which music can be provided for in the primary school, which has the potential to alter the way music learning is provided for quite profoundly.

New technologies are always appearing and so teachers are faced with the task of keeping abreast of what technology can do and what it can't do. It might be helpful to make a distinction between two different learning purposes for technologies. The first purpose is to extend the musical resources, give access to a wider range of sounds and musical possibilities which in turn connect to a wider range of musical styles. The second purpose is to provide a set of learning approaches which can add to children's learning in every area of musical activity. These learning approaches will link with technology using skills common to other areas of the curriculum – computing skills, investigation skills etc. From the ICT side, music provides a distinctive set of approaches through which ICT competences can be developed.

As an extended musical source, technologies offer a wider range of musical materials far beyond the sound possibilities which can be produced by the usual instrumental technology of classroom percussion instruments. These sounds are thrilling to the ear and aural imagination. Who has not started out with a keyboard by first pressing every sound just for sheer delight in the timbres? The sound sources of keyboards and computers can run in to hundreds of pre-sets. Record and replay facilities allow music to be played even faster, even slower than children could perform it. Amplifications can make it ear-deafeningly loud or almost inaudibly softer. Added effects can change and distort the timbre. Sounds can be doubled, textures thickened or made squeaky thin. The sound can disappear into cassettes, computer discs, down headphones and across splitters only to reappear when wanted. Electronically produced sounds bring timbres which connect specifically to pop, rock, new age, electroacoustic musics and many more. What is more, these are sounds and music which are 'here and now'. Children as they become older in primary schools will find it increasingly difficult to relate to school music if it sounds out of touch with a contemporary music world beyond school which beckons.

Music technologies allow children to learn differently. Most fundamentally they encourage individual, partner or small group work and more self-directed activity than is traditionally possible in a whole-class music session. While there may be times when everyone as a class can usefully come together for a listening or an explanation around a piece of equipment, on the whole work will be individual. As such, it requires different things of the teacher whose role is now to support the self-directed activity with the appropriate strategies.

The emphasis upon individual activity is not just a practical one because equipment is expensive and has to be shared in turns, it brings bonuses to children's learning. Technology can free children from the limitations of their own performance skills. It can either take the music children make themselves on instruments and do much more with it, beyond the scope of their own performance skills, or it can provide the musical materials from the start. Sound crafting in many different ways becomes possible. And just as in art work or writing, crafting with materials is best done alone. The processes of working with sound demand sharp aural awareness and making aural choices, imagining modifications and working towards refinement. These are the processes which lie at the heart of what music is all about and so are central to its education. Technologies can make a vital contribution to these fundamental learning processes.

Because music happens over time, memory skills are essential. Children's composition is often limited by the children's ability to recall their ideas, either from moment to moment as they explore them or from session to session. Technology can record and play back instantly both to assist children's memory learning and to allow longer and more complex ideas to be developed in their work. Saving work can be easily achieved on cassettes, video or computer disk so that children are freed of the need to work only with what can be remembered or notated in some form. Some programs will convert music into notation which can then be printed off.

There are disadvantages to using music technologies in teaching. Each of these music tools discussed in this chapter will do some things well and some less well and being clear about these is part of the teachers' task in collecting a repertoire of approaches to suit all music learning purposes. One of the disadvantages of technology is that music in some senses belongs to the body, not to machinery. Ready-made or easy-to-produce sound materials may free children from the physical actions of making many of the sounds on instruments or with voices themselves. And this brings the added advantage that children can listen in a detached way without also having to produce the sounds simultaneously. But without the physical feel of the instrument or voice and how the sound is made, children are losing out on an important source of understanding. Knowledge about music is not built from aural information alone, bodily action makes an important contribution. Drum pads, floor pads, even the small rubber preset pads on a keyboard which require children to still physically 'play' to produce the sound can compensate for the mechanisation process. Another approach is to integrate, as far as possible, acoustic instruments and digital technology by for example picking up the sounds with microphones, transducers, recordings to become the sound materials for working. These two approaches draw together learning advantages from both sides of the body or machine quandary.

Digital technologies allow for the storage and retrieval of information on a scale fantastically beyond anything which has been possible with paper and printing technologies. Multimedia, providing simultaneous sight and sound, will prove to be an invaluable learning medium for music education. Both CD ROMs and the Internet provide opportunities for children to follow and research their own interests and needs.

Music software in the form of music games and composing programs is now commonplace in many schools. Computer music programs still mostly have a basic computer games format built in with brightly coloured graphics, such as pictures, standing in for snippets of tune. The challenges of win-or-lose situations are often lightweight and teachers will analyse carefully what music learning is being gained. The tasks are in many cases reduced to narrow prescription and the opportunities for individual contribution are minimal. On the plus side, the computer can act as tutor offering time-intensive practice at basic skills, perhaps listening skills, and it does offer individually paced learning and immediate feedback. For example, computer programs are in development which will give children an immediate visual feedback on their voice pitching skills. There is also the opportunity for guided home-work, when children take the discs home (this assumes a compatible home-computer).

Working with technology alters time patterns for learning, in some ways compressing time and in some ways stretching it out in long spans. Push-button immediacy speeds up many processes. Each new thing tumbles out in brief stop-go snatches. Some children can keep pace with the faster tempo of thinking, others are overwhelmed by the information expansion and much by-passes them. From observation teachers need to decide whether to intervene in order to slow down and focus the child's working or to leave them working as they are. It is easy for a fascination with technology to take over and for the musical processes to be lost. For example, in working with a keyboard the teacher might focus the child by setting a structured task with built-in limitations. At other times working with technology needs long stretches of time. If skills are not to remain at a low-level, considerable time may be required at key points to move the child on to further understanding and competence. Any adult who is self-taught to use a computer can recognise the way in which sometimes we simply need to stay with one thing. Children must have time to explore equipment if they are to apply it constructively to new musical situations. Allowing for a spill-over of time one day may be time-efficient in the long run. To provide for longer working times, turn-taking may run slowly across a whole term rather than in ten-minute turnabouts. Flexibility on the part of the teacher is important to allow for these kinds of time structuring. A five-minute burst with a quick pace music game might be just enough, a three hour session extending into after school time may be necessary to work on a composition. (See page 122 for a further discussion of time for working in music.)

Very few teachers have background training in music technologies, although technological literacy is increasing all round. The first stage is self-education. This may entail feeling comfortable with incompetence, seeking out others to learn from and making the learning time a priority, built into the music development plan. If value is placed on integrating aspects of technology then time is found. Perhaps, for example, the end of term concert is replaced by an open evening at which children work with and demonstrate the new equipment and their growing competencies.

Because music technologies are relatively new into primary education there has been little research into how children's learning is affected by their use. Classteachers are at the forefront of innovations and so practice-based action research is vital. Observation of children and noting everything they do is important. If possible the notes might be discussed with another teacher and then analysed to separate out those observations which are connected with music learning and those which are connected with learning to use the equipment itself. Observations collected over time from a number of children may begin to reveal general strategies the children employ and suggest ways in which in future the work might be structured or guided by the teacher. These findings could then be disseminated to other staff in the school, beyond the school on teachers' courses or an e-mail network of music coordinators, added to discussion pages on the Internet, written about in magazines and journals for teachers.

equipment

Where does the teacher make a start with music technologies? A suggested starting point is to extend the range of acoustic sounds by pick-up through microphone or transducer and then modifying them through amplifiers, echo machines. Starting equipment might be:

- microphone and stand;
- amplifier;
- plate microphone; *to pick up sounds from an area wider than the usual microphone, can be placed flat on the table or floor;*
- transducer; *small, thin disc attached to an audio plug which is connected to amplifier and will pick up specific sounds;*
- echo machine; *a small box which is then plugged into the*

amplifier, can be adjusted to produce echoes with varying delays;

Another starting point is to work with electronically produced sounds. Keyboards are the obvious producer of electronical sounds. Some of the sounds are imitations of known instruments and some are simulated sounds. Simulated percussion sounds can be produced on keyboard pads. Many keyboards are equipped with memory facilities and sequencer (a recording facility which will repeat sounds over and over to make drone or ostinati effects).

Computer software is available which records sound from a keyboard directly linked by MIDI and then allows that sound to be modified by the computer programme.

music notebooks

The idea of each child keeping a sketchbook is fairly well established in art work and working books are used in other curriculum areas, language, maths, DT, for example. These notebooks, sketchbooks or workbooks – what they are called is less important than the way they are used – have many connecting and overlapping functions and purposes. They are a place to store children's work so that individual pathways of progress can be tracked by children themselves, teacher and parents. They are a place to collect ideas and then begin to explore them so that ways of working which are process-based and creative are fostered and supported (Robinson, 1995). In an art notebook, for example, the child is encouraged to collect and keep samples of visual ideas, both found and researched, as a store of ideas which can feed into later working. In a workbook for language, thoughts and words are jotted and may be reworked in writing processes of drafting and editing.

It is very important that the notebook is the child's own and is allowed to evolve according to the child's own interests and enthusiasms. As a result it becomes highly personal to the child, recording achievements and struggles, and the unfolding of their own musical identity. Keeping a notebook can raise children's level of involvement and motivation and this has a knock-on effect upon the quality of their learning.

A music notebook is a place where the child can:
- gather their own aural ideas and thoughts;
- generate ideas for their own work by reworking what is gathered;
- store their own compositions and work in progress;
- make responses to musical experiences;
- keep a record of repertoire played and sung or listened to;
- collect samples of music, (recorded and notated) and information about music which interests them;
- keep exercises activities for skill practising and practice notes;
- make notes about their progress and plans for what to do next;
- work at set tasks.

The descriptions which follow give some images of the ways in which notebooks might support music learning:
- Jason in Year 3 takes a turn to work on his composition using the xylophone set up in the entrance-way to his classroom. He fetches his music notebook in which during his last turn of working he had written some short melody ideas in a simple form using letter names from the keys of the xylophone. First he reads this back, they remind him of his melodic ideas and then he can continue.

- Jasmin and Hafsa in Year 5 are working together to learn a song they have chosen from a tape provided in their class songbook. When they have learnt the song to be able to sing it independently, they record their performance on tape and make a note of their activity in their notebooks, adding comments on how they managed the learning of the song.

First thoughts might be that for each child to keep an individual notebook for music is impractical, one more thing to manage when teachers are already hard-pressed enough. Yet in contrast to children's work in other areas of the curriculum which is usually kept with care and respect, a child's music work, all too often, disappears without trace. There are, after all, particular problems associated with collecting and keeping music. But progress grows from what has gone before, and if what has gone before is always lost in a climate of instant and disposable music-making then there is little chance of building a sense of real progression and continuity.

The storing of musical ideas and music work in progress is likely to include some recording on cassette, video or computer disk. If equipment is limited, there is the added task of coordinating systems for sharing. These are not the only methods for saving musical ideas, for useful detail can be jotted on paper in the form of words, diagrams, drawings, notations, annotated lyrics, instrument fingerings and computer specifications. In all, the music notebook might contain:

- ideas for composing: *written in words and notations;*
- details of compositions in progress or completed: *with reference to work saved on audio/video tape or to notations;*
- references to musical ideas gathered from listening: *on cassettes/CDs in the listening library, to other children's music, to known songs or instrumental pieces;*
- graphic scores, notations of own music or music of others: *self-produced, printed off from computer etc.;*

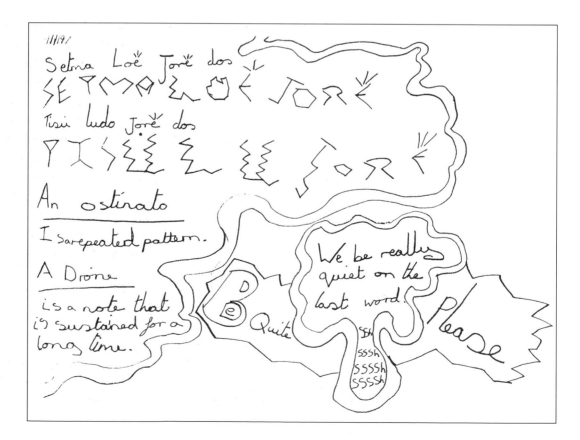

- written comments: *relating to samples of own work saved on audio/video tape e.g. about singing development;*
- investigations of music: *written in words, diagrams, notations;*
- written accounts of musical experiences: *e.g. of performances, their own or given by others;*
- interviews: *with other children, family, other adults about musical issues;*
- written information: *about the time or place of songs, music learnt for playing or music listened to etc.;*
- information from the Internet: *favourite web sites, print-outs from web-sites, e-mails;*
- instructions: *e.g. how to play instruments, details about fingerings, chord patterns etc., information about how to use ICT equipment etc.;*
- exercises: *to practise skill learning – listening awareness, voice or instrumental skills;*
- diary: *for homework, for practice schedules;*
- records: *of songs learnt, of range of ICT activities, of instrumental skills acquired etc.*

In the early stages children are likely to need help in learning how to use their books most effectively and will need nudging in certain directions. Gathering and collecting musical ideas will depend in part upon children having words and other ways of translating musical ideas into written forms. Teachers will anticipate this need, either by giving a specific lead input or by recognising when a child's work demonstrates that they need to know, for example, specific terms or ways of notating. Children will require assistance in learning audio or video recording techniques on different kinds of equipment. Not every piece of music work will be recorded in some way: the decision whether to save or not and in what form can be made with the child. Investment in the early days to develop effective ways of using the music workbook and proficiency with saving and retrieval techniques (which will overlap with ICT competency) will pay off in the long run as children develop increasing independence.

In the later stages of primary schooling children are able to carry out the processes of storing and retrieving their music work independently, leaving the teacher free to concentrate on taking an overview role and on taking time to confer with children about their work in progress. Towards the end of primary schooling extracts from the music notebooks can form part of an audio display for parents' evenings. Finally, the progress and review pages can be separated out from the loose ringbinder along with some samples of significant achievement to carry over at the point of transfer into secondary schooling.

making the notebook

While ready-made books could be used, a flexible system of a binder or folder to which pages can be added offers more opportunity for children to gather up in their notebook all kinds of pages, pre-printed, photocopied, computer print-outs and their own notations. Home-made books can also incorporate pocket pages in the cover for cassettes and/or computer disks. With older children the loose-leaf system in which they can add pages to a binder or folder works successfully (and allows key pages to be later taken out and passed on to next classes/schools). With younger children, larger sized books in which the pages are laced together are practical or, alternatively, ready-made books for working in directly with any additions pasted in.

The following details give more precise suggestions:
- a plastic side binder: *A4 size cut (sawed) in half gives a more manageable A5 size booklet;*
- two A5 card covers: *with a stapled pocket on the inside of the front cover for one cassette tape or computer disk and special place on inside back cover for parents' comments;*
- blank A5 pages: *for children to use as they choose, to make jottings when working on composing, to collect ideas and thoughts about music made or listened to etc.;*
- pre-printed A5 pages with headings and columns for specific purposes: e.g.
  listening reviews;
  pages for recording performance repertoire (songs or instrumental pieces);
  set tasks;
  end of term progress reviews;
- task pages: e.g.
  instrumental or vocal skill activities;
  homework instructions;

notation activities;
starter ideas for composition;
● score pages: e.g.
child-made – of compositions or known music learnt aurally;
of songs or instrumental pieces;
sample pages of music listened to.

The notebook is best kept inside a larger envelope folder which also houses large size music copies, computer disks, video and cassette tapes. Ideally each child will have two short length cassette tapes, one as a rough working tape and another which contains only work which the child wants to keep long-term. On their 'best' tape, check the children are keeping a careful note of where each item is. (Many a composition has been lost by inadvertently copying over.) Suppliers offer loose cassettes without cases more economically – children can make their own packet and include a listing of recorded 'numbers'.

investigating music

primary music: later years

What kinds of things are there to be investigated in music? Roughly, they might be divided into two groups:

- things about how the music itself is constructed; *this includes all the detail of how the elements of pitch, duration, timbre, texture, and dynamics are brought together as melody, rhythm, and musical patterns and forms;*
- things about how the music is or was made, improvised or composed, and about its purposes and social and cultural context; *this includes all the detail about the people who make or made the music and about how it relates to the musical practices of a particular style, culture, time or place.*

In fact, of course, these two groups are inseparable. How music is constructed always relates to how and why and in what context it is made; understanding either without reference to the other is meaningless. Blacking (1987) writes: 'Musical ideas are human constructs that are related to other ideas in cultural systems'; his work across music of different cultures explores in detail ways in which this may be so. Investigating these things with children, and ensuring that children themselves know how to become interested, and to ask, investigate and discover is one of the most powerful ways of making music directly accessible to them.

investigating skills

How do you investigate something that's invisible? that won't keep still? that disappears as it unfolds? and that can't be got hold of all at once even when you've come to know it quite well? How do you investigate something that requires elaborate technology if it is to be captured and transported from one place or time to another? What if that technology wasn't or isn't available – if we know something existed but can never know exactly what it was like *then*…or *there*…? if we would need to transport ourselves into some other life, in a very different world, in order to get an inside experience of it?

Involving children in investigating music brings us face to face with these hazards, just as they are encountered by performers, critics and researchers working with all kinds of music. And it is the characteristic elusiveness of the actual musical sound, like the materials of any time-based art, which makes investigation fascinating, if at times frustrating. At its best, learning about music of different times and places is exploratory, adventurous and surprising. Making musical discoveries therefore requires a combination of skills ranging from acute and analytical listening, using musical memory, imagination, empathy and responsiveness, to skills of finding and using sources of information, critical thinking in applying findings to the music itself, and using approaches to problem-solving as new questions arise. A stimulating learning environment for music is characterised by the excitement of opening up more and more possibilities for knowledge and understanding and by the growing confidence of teachers and pupils in their own powers to do this. An approach to music which is essentially investigative, critical and questioning establishes a positive learning climate and can become an integral part of all work in music, whether composing, performing, listening or appraising.

Most children are enthusiastic investigators once their interest is aroused. Teachers who approach musical knowledge in such a way that the processes of questioning, hypothesising, researching and applying findings are modelled and shared with pupils are likely to arouse interest and heighten children's motivation to learn. In this respect music is no different from other curriculum areas such as history, science and geography. Ensuring that children's own investigating skills are developed as part of the music curriculum is vital. To a considerable extent these skills are transferable across the curriculum anyway, but they are often under-used in music, where there is a tradition of teachers handing on information rather than combining this with engaging learners in research.

The research approach is particularly significant in ensuring that pupils become aware and informed composers and performers, who can begin to understand their own music making in the context of much wider musical experience and knowledge. Ultimately, once skills and interest have been developed, children can continue to apply this approach to any music they sing, play or listen to within school or beyond. It is important, therefore, that investigating music does not become a separate activity of its own. Rather, linked with listening and appraising, it becomes an aspect of any musical activity – whether composing, performing, improvising or being an audience for live or recorded performance. Investigative skills are best developed as opportunities arise which make them most meaningful and useful. For example:

● A class who have been practising singing a folk song with a local reference receive a visit from a local folk performer who sings this and other songs associated with the region with them. The children ask questions, some of which they've prepared with the class teacher beforehand, to find out more about 'their' song. Later, the song is entered on the world map which is kept for recording the place of origin of music sung, played, listened or danced to during the year. The song has a verse and chorus structure: two children are asked to collect more examples of songs with verse and chorus and compare the word and tune patterns, reporting back to everyone. Finally, the class together work out the set of notes the tune is based on, singing the note set as a scale; two children go on to explore it further by using it for their own songs.

● Extracts from Vivaldi's *Winter and Spring* from *The Four Seasons* have been heard again recently in assembly, introduced in relation to the coming of spring. The Year 6 class teacher holds a brief discussion afterwards to find out what anybody knows about :
i)   Vivaldi
ii) violins
iii) violin (or other) concertos
iv) this piece of music: *The Four Seasons*.
The assembled discussion jottings are very thin. There is some first-hand information from two children who learn the violin about how it is played and that the music sounded quite hard. There is general agreement that the music probably is hard as it has quite a few twiddles even in the slow bits. There is also some agreement that Vivaldi sounds like a Spanish name.

A second discussion quickly establishes a much longer list of questions that could be asked and things it would be interesting to know. Suggestions are taken with each question as to how it might be answered and some pairs of children are allocated the task of finding more about one thing each to report back in time for a further hearing of the music next week. Time is minimal and this is to be done whenever a few minutes can be found. Sources are restricted to: the CD cover notes, a book on composers in the library, another recording of Vivaldi's music found in the school collection, the violin teacher and the reception teacher who had chosen the music that day.

By the time the music is next heard, it has been established, among other things that Vivaldi was an early 18th century Italian composer who wrote a great deal of his music for performance by the girls and young women of an orphanage convent school in Venice, where he taught violin and directed the music. The violin pupils have brought some more information about the violin techniques used and how, in Vivaldi's time, this was a relatively new instrument and often used for virtuoso music which allowed players to show off their skills. The idea of concertos in which one instrument is set against a large group has been discussed and other kinds of contrast, such as loud followed by quieter music, are noticed.

In each of the above cases, familiarity with a small amount of music has been capitalised on by staying with the pieces a bit longer and opening up investigation around them. Pooling resources by sharing small investigations of different kinds around the class adds interest, and a varied set of sources has been drawn on. All this helps to bring together a considerable amount of knowledge as well as extending understanding as children try to piece together the 'story' as a whole. In the second case, the opening discussion gathers up a rough picture first and then uses this as a basis for formulating questions. This models a process which gives children confidence in making their own hypotheses and then finding ways to translate them into firmer knowledge.

developing skills

The skills inherent in investigative work are not easily separated out from each other. Much of the learning rests on a synthesis of the different ways we have of gaining access to musical insight and information. Bringing together what is known about some music with what is actually heard and experienced is a process which in itself takes practice. Through the later primary years children become able to move towards skill development of this second-order kind as their ability to think analytically about time-based structures, to make sense of style and to conceptualise and use language as a questioning and research tool increases.

Given consistent and appropriate opportunities during the early years, by the age of 7 most children will have learnt how to give concentrated listening attention to music they hear, dance to, sing or play. They will be able to describe what they hear in simple terms and to talk about music in different ways. They will have begun to investigate how music is put together and to learn to ask questions about its background, purpose and context. And they will have some initial experience of using people, pictures, books and computers as resources for finding out. For children who lack such a basis, these must be the starting points (Young and Glover, 1998) and it may be a while before they are ready to go further, particularly in becoming more independent. In this case, investigating activities taken as a class, with the teacher modelling approaches and children's ideas pooled and built on, will be the most useful format while listening skills, vocabulary and ways of beginning to investigate are established.

Building on this foundation, development of investigative skills during the later primary years is characterised mainly by the extension of each aspect, and a growing independence in application of skills leading to more individualised interpretations and understanding. In addition, one or two new skill areas come into operation. Bearing in mind that in practice these skills are inter-related, the following outline indicates how capabilities may be extended over this middle age-phase.

giving listening attention, staying with the music

Following music as a listener in a way that is concentrated and stays with the music as it develops is not easy. It is a skill which has to be practised. Although quite young children can listen to extended pieces of music, their ability to do so depends on how much experience they have of focused listening. Teachers can have high expectations and work at this kind of listening explicitly with the children. It is a pre-requisite for investigation of the music itself.

Gene Lees, writing a sleeve note to a track of Bill Evans' jazz piano music, says: 'You will hear this track for the first time only once. And though it grows more beautiful with repeated hearings, there is in it … some sense of unfolding discovery that is there *only* the first time you hear it.' As children become more able to discuss listening processes with awareness, they can learn to stage their listening in different ways: the first hearing just for the impact, the next to see what else strikes you, the next for a particular aspect of the music – the running bass line, the recurring idea – and so on. A distinction can be made between listening for detail and listening for the overall effect; different strategies can be chosen as needed.

listening awareness

The skills of listening have been discussed in earlier sections. It is important that investigating music does not become something that is done only through books and other indirect sources. Finding out how music works by listening is irreplaceable; being told how it works is no substitute, however much this may open up new perspectives. A major task for this age phase is to teach children to trust their ears and to begin to think analytically about what they hear going on in the music. This rests on using their developing understanding of musical elements and runs alongside developing confidence in language use. Initially, children can be encouraged to talk and write about first hand musical discoveries made in this way.

After listening to an extract from Michael Nyman's music for Prospero's Books (1991, Decca CD 425 224-2), children commented:

> 'The woodwind played the melody'.
> 'The piano chords were underneath. The chord changes and it is playing up and down.'
> 'High voice, strings, piano – 3 layers'. 'I didn't like the high female voice.'
> 'It gets louder towards the end.' 'There's an unusual sudden finish.'

Such descriptions form the basis for moving on to more reflective and analytical comment, some of which begins to emerge here. As experience widens, children can begin to hypothesise about the music on the basis of what they hear, relating it to other music encountered.

Listening to music from Mozambique, a small group tried to work out where it came from, each having a different idea:

'It could be from Mexico – it's got lots of skin drums.'
'Africa – I've heard some children who sing like this.'
'Jamaica – it sounds like Jamaican drums.'
'It could be played outside in a field, in the dust, when it's dark.'

These children are focusing primarily on the instrumental sound; a next stage is to refer to other musical features, such as rhythm and melody too. Children's capacity for recognising and placing musical style increases enormously during this age-phase; teachers can help children to develop the listening skills which underpin this.

using notations

A relatively small proportion of music belongs to traditions in which notation is embedded. Where this is so, reference to musical scores in conjunction with listening can yield a surprising amount of information, even where children haven't yet the literacy skills to read them fully. It can be well worth borrowing from the library scores of music being investigated and treating them almost like artefacts to be examined. Children can be encouraged to look closely, make observations and then relate these to the sound of the music. The beginning or end of a piece is easiest to match up, but by the upper end of the age group, some children at least are able to follow a score while the music plays if it is reasonably straightforward.

Notations are, to a greater or lesser extent, visual analogues of musical sound. Texture, for instance, is immediately made visible through most kinds of notations; the page is more or less black and cluttered. Similarly, traditional rhythm notations look very different if there are lots of short notes or a few much longer ones. Facsimiles of composers' hand-written manuscripts can also be fascinating to children – neat or untidy, with many or few corrections.

speaking and listening

As indicated above, people are an excellent source of information and insight. There are many kinds of music, particularly contemporary musics of all kinds, where there is relatively little written. In any case, a personal perspective always adds another invaluable dimension to the communication of knowledge.

As the language skills of speaking and listening develop, they can be brought to bear in investigating music. Learning to formulate questions, interviewing someone with and without prepared questions, listening to their contributions, and debating different viewpoints are general language skills which can be practised as well in the musical context as in any other. Conversations can be one-to-one or whole class events; with permission, they can be taped and referred to later or listened to as talking books. Even short (arranged) telephone conversations can contribute exciting additional findings to an investigation.

reading skills, using written sources of information

At seven, children's ability to use written sources of information is limited and dependent on those sources being simple enough for them to read. By eleven, many pupils are able to use adult reference texts in addition to resources specially produced for primary school reference. Expectations of children's ability to investigate music from written sources has obviously to keep pace with this enormous change, whilst allowing for those who still have difficulties to work at their own level.

The independence which comes from knowing how to find out, and having the skills to use written texts to do so is of value in itself. More than this, though it opens musical doors which are often left closed simply by default, but leaving an impression that musical knowledge is somehow out of reach. Learning to find a book, use a contents page or index, look up an item alphabetically and make a notebook entry summarising findings, not only affords practise in these general skills, but gives a sense of the presence of a world of musical knowledge alongside that of other areas.

ICT skills using CD ROM and Internet

An extension of the use of reading skills is in their similar applications with information technology. CD ROMs as reference material have the unique advantage of offering musical sound as well as words and pictures and the multi-media revolution has had probably more impact in music than in most areas. Similarly, as schools are becoming linked to the Internet, the potential for searching for and finding information with sound as well as text is expanding all the time. E-mail exchanges offer immediate and cheap access across distance and can make opportunities for two-way exchange and collaborations between schools and pupils, as well as an additional source of information or personal comment.

The motivation for children in researching music through technology is strong, and their level of competence during this age phase reaches the point at which they can enjoy pursuing a quest, controlling choices of sources, and having access to musical examples in sound which can be listened to repeatedly.

use of visual materials

As in history, children learn to use paintings, reproductions, photographs, and artefacts as further sources of information, developing skills of looking, questioning, evaluating what such representations suggest, and drawing conclusions from them, so these skills can be applied and practised in order to learn more about the musical practice of other times and places. Using such sources with a degree of awareness about their limitations in terms of accuracy holds valuable lessons in itself; an imaginative dimension can be added to this by asking children to look at a painting or carving of people making music and think how it might have sounded.

recording and display of findings

Investigations can be tracked and the results recorded at both a personal level and as part of a larger project drawing contributions together from a group or class. Children can keep journal entries in music notebooks as investigations move forward and these can record personal reflections and reactions alongside factual findings and description.

Communicating findings offers a whole range of possibilities for collating materials and presenting discoveries, questions and comment in a variety of media, for example:

- visual displays on wall in classroom or more public space;
- audio or video taped presentations combining music and dialogue, with visual material on tape or accompanying;
- 'live' presentations to own or another class or in assembly, with visual aids, music and perhaps drama;
- a collated book to be kept in the school library;
- a file on disc to be accessed by computer.

providing for investigating

In practical terms, to support an investigative approach to listening and performing, a school can work towards the following:

- value listening; invest in good quality sound equipment in every classroom: CD players and a listening base with headphones and splitters for individual and small group listening; if this seems unreasonable, ask whether conditions for listening to music in the classroom shouldn't at least match those in most homes; include access to a multi-media computer, with Internet if possible;

- collect plenty of music reference books; monitor these to ensure a coverage of music of different times, places and styles, of classical, folk, jazz, pop, religious and world music, of male and female composers and performers, of musicians of all kinds across a range of ethnic origins; include some adult reference books;

- collect other reference sources e.g. art books, CD ROM , museum and exhibition catalogues, artefacts, musical scores;

- identify staff special interests and seek out other people who are willing to visit, show, talk and be questioned about any particular aspect of music or related topics;

- link performing with listening to recorded music as much as possible; hearing how other performers make music helps in developing performing skills and a sense of style; recorded performances are reference material in themselves;

- encourage a whole school approach to investigating music: expect children to be as specific and detailed as possible in researching particular pieces of music; cover less ground if necessary but allow children to get inside the piece and its context and to use a range of sources of information.

early music

The following investigations are intended to show a range of practical approaches which might be taken to any historical music, or to music of different places and cultures. Here they are applied to examples of music from the European middle ages and the English Tudor period.

Early music is a rather broad term. In one very real sense this music is not particularly early or old at all. Much older major civilisations such as the Egyptians and Aztecs had their own musical traditions; and today there are many cultures with much longer unbroken musical traditions than this, for example, Chinese or Arabic traditions. As far as we can tell music is as old as human society. The music which is referred to as 'early music' from a contemporary perspective – in early music festivals, on radio, in magazines and record shops, – belongs to the earlier kinds of European music for which there are surviving notations in manuscript and other documentary evidence of how the music might have been played or sung – treatises, letters, illustrations. The dependence on notation narrows the field considerably, both in kind and quantity of music represented. Most historical music will remain lost until a method is found of picking up the sonic vibrations of previous times.

For many of today's early music performers, much of the interest rests in seeing a whole process through from finding and editing manuscripts to performing the music and bringing it alive for audiences. This process combines scholarship and research with performance and engages a curiosity and motivation to discover and solve problems which is shared by historians and detectives; it also raises issues which are hotly debated. When performing music of the past, should the performer try to recreate the music as it would have originally been heard? If so, how can we discover what it sounded like? Should 'authentic' instruments be used, reconstructed to be as like the originals as possible? Should methods of voice production, of singing style, of ornamentation be recreated? How much can we know of these when they were part of an understood performance practice of the day, not needing to be defined or described in writings? What happens where there is no indication in notation of the rhythm of the music because manuscripts were not for performance or where rhythmic interpretation was another understood practice? These are live issues for performers and they easily catch children's imaginations too. If there were no ways of recording sound, how would people in the year 3000 know what our music sounded like?

Then there are other musical questions for performers which draw attention to the processes of interpreting music. What happens when there is conflict between trying to recreate music 'authentically' and our own musical taste and response, for example when *it would have been played like this, but I prefer it like that?* Do we refer to how things were or to the original makers' intentions? Supposing the composer would have preferred the sound of more modern instruments if they'd been available? The approaches to performance pioneered in the field of very early music have now permeated attitudes to the performance of classical music into the early twentieth century. A performer might choose to play eighteenth or nineteenth century piano music on period instruments by particular makers. Both the investigation and the debates help to raise awareness of fine detail in differences of historical and geographical style.

All this lends itself very much as an approach to historical music with children. Approaches taken to history in the curriculum emphasise investigation, finding and using evidence, evaluating sources, imagination and empathy. Music of other times takes on a more vivid reality when it is investigated in an exploratory way, when it is seen in the wider context of society and its domestic or public functions. Thinking about choices performers have to make in relation to what they know about a piece, and that taking into account style and period can aid decisions about interpretation, helps children gain insight into performing as a whole. Music isn't just there: it has to be made, created, and this always involves decision making. The above questions can be raised and discussed with children:

- to widen understanding of the active role of listeners and performers;
- to give children confidence to question and research;
- to encourage them to use their artistic judgment.

planning points

This general approach can be used to introduce listening to and/or performing single pieces of music as 'one-offs' or can run in a more extended way as a music topic or alongside a half term history topic. Across the 7–11 age-range, children should become familiar with music from a range of different times and places; this will gradually build into a wider picture of historical and world music and a developing sense of musical style. It is important to allow enough time for chosen pieces to be heard lots of times and to find their way into a class listening repertoire from which selections are revisited, just as stories and books might be. Recordings of music introduced to the class as a whole can be kept in a class or school listening library for individual listening on headphones at the listening centre. Performing any historical music can be linked to listening to other examples. A wall-poster sized time-line and map are good ways to chart listening and performing repertoire so that children can begin to make sense of the sound of musical styles and genres in relation to historical or geographical context. Children will keep notes of their investigations and their responses in music notebooks and draw on these in relation to performing and composing. A repertoire log to move on with each class to the next teacher helps to avoid overlap and to keep breadth and balance in view.

Whether or not the teacher has extensive knowledge of a particular piece or style of music is often less important than the approach they enable children to adopt. The aim is for children to become informed and critical listeners and performers and independent learners. A teacher who can foster these approaches will open children's access to much greater musical knowledge and understanding than one who tells a short story about the composer, instrument or occasion and then puts on the CD. If unsure, early music is a good place to start; pieces are often smaller in scale and clear-cut and vivid to listen to.

The following examples are intended as indications only of the kinds of investigations that might arise from different starting points and skill bases.

music for the spirit: Hildegard of Bingen

There is an extraordinary level of general interest in Hildegard, a 12th century German abbess, who lived in a convent on the Rhine. Although she appears little in medieval music history books (to their discredit), a great deal of her music is extant in the Hessiche Landesbibliothek at Weisbaden and there are innumerable recordings of her music, in both 'authentic' and more creative versions.

Located on a time line of early women composers, Hildegard appears among the earliest:

c.810-c.843	1098-1179	1480-1530	1507-1536	1540-1590	1587-c.1636	1619-1664	1667-1729
Kassia	Hildegard von Bingen	Margaret of Austria	Anne Boleyn	Casulana	Francesca Caccini	Strozzi	Jacque de la Guerre
		c.1160 Comtesse de Dia		c.1570-1646 V and R Aleotti		1620-1704 Leonarda	c.1640-50 Cozzolani

Time line of early women composers

Across nine centuries she seems to speak to something in contemporary experience, not least in her holistic outlook and breadth of expertise across theology, medicine, music, politics and environmental interests. Literally a visionary, the illuminated manuscripts of her inspirations are works of art in themselves (Fox, 1985). Her work lends itself to investigation across a whole range of disciplines.

Hildegard's music belongs to a tradition of unaccompanied plainchant and the pieces are examples of this in a free style. Investigation is best begun by listening with eyes closed, allowing the music to take effect in its own terms and without discussion. Choose a recording of any of her music in one of the more authentic versions e.g. a track from *Canticles of Ecstasy* or *Voice of the Blood*, recorded by the group Sequentia. A listening–led investigation of the music might then go on to:

activities

~ Trace the melodic shape of the music in the air with your hand; try to stay with every twist and turn in the music; describe the kind of melody you are hearing; perhaps draw some of it on paper; *listening attention, staying with the music, focus on element of pitch.*

~ Discuss what kind of building this music might belong to, and what setting in place and time; use your imagination to picture the people who first made this music; *speculating, considering context, using language.*

~ Hildegard often uses small fragments of melody which are used several times in music that is otherwise quite free. One of these 'thumb-prints' is moving from a low D, via A to a high D and then coming down by step. Try singing this and listen out for it. Do you notice any other examples in the music?

〜 The manuscript in which the music is written down (for facsimile of *'Ordo virtutum'* see Ekdahl Davidson, 1992) was used to keep a record of the music but does not tell performers what time-lengths, rhythm or tempo to use. Discuss how the performers you have heard interpret the rhythm; *analysing performance aspects, using language about duration.*

Investigation can subsequently broaden to finding out more about Hildegard and her music (Pugh, 1991, Sadie and Samuel, 1994). Or it can lead into composing, using some of the characteristics of her music.

music for processions: *The Play of Daniel*

To the all-powerful holder of the stars this crowd of men and boys offers praise.

This 13th century tune lends itself well to investigating through performing. A small or large group of singers and/or instrumentalists can learn the tune and play it for others to listen or, in dramatic context, to try out as a processional. Performers can play from notation or decode the pitches and learn the tune by heart. Children who can read the notation can 'translate' for others.

The music is an example of a *conductus*, a processional song used in medieval Christian churches. Processions formed part of many ceremonies – from church to church, from one altar to another within the church, or for the arrival and departure of priests and clergy. *The Play of Daniel*, from which the piece comes, is one of the oldest surviving pieces of music drama and has an introduction indicating that it was performed by young monks in Beauvais Cathedral, most likely as part of the celebrations of the Feast of Fools, shortly after Christmas. The manuscript is in the British Museum (MS Egerton 2615). This conductus forms the opening procession, during which the Biblical story of Daniel is outlined. The play contains other conducti, with annotated stage directions such as 'Balshazzar coming to the Palace' or 'Daniel coming to the King'.

The melody has been transcribed from the original and moved four notes lower, from G to D as the starting note, in order to make it a better pitch for voices. As with Hildegard's music, the manuscript gives pitches only. The rhythm of the text and the repeating note patterns, typical of conducti, suggests that the rhythm suggested above the text could be used all through. It is unclear whether instruments would have accompanied the singing or not. If instruments are to be used they can:

- play the melody;
- add a drone, on D;
- add a drum beat or pattern.

activities

↝ Learn to sing and/or play the tune. Discuss whether the pitch is a good one, change it if not. Discuss whether the rhythm pattern works for a procession. What speed does the beat need to be if people are to move while singing?

↝ Hum the tune through in your mind. Discuss what you notice about the range of notes and how the melody moves by step or by jump. Think about where to breathe to make sense of these shapes. How easy is it for a voice to perform?

↝ Look at the Latin text and agree how to pronounce it so that diction can be clear. Look at the translation to find out that this is a song of praise.

↝ What strategies can be used for a group of singers and players to keep in time without a conductor? Think about the listening involved and try ideas out.

The note set from which this melody is built is DEFGA C' D'.
Listen to and look at the melody closely. The tune is built as if it rests on D.
The note set is a Dorian mode, which would include a B natural if needed.

➰ Compose a processional tune using this mode. Decide on the kind of mood or occasion the procession might be for.

Investigation can go on to finding out more about *The Play of Daniel* and the story on which it is based and listening to more of the music. Or it could turn to finding other music designed for processions of different kinds e.g. the Entrance music for the Emperor of China, dated c. 1000BC, and probably played by literally hundreds of instrumentalists, in unison, on zithers, lutes, mouth organs, oboes, drums, bells and chimes (Davison and Apel, 1946).

● ───

music for entertainment: *In nomine* by Robert Parsons

Among its enormous collection of music manuscripts, the British Museum holds books of music which would have been played and sung for domestic entertainment in the homes of wealthy English families, from royalty down. Investigating this music with the help of facsimiles of the original manuscripts can link understanding of the music itself to its place in the lives of those who made it.

The example given here, reproduced by permission of the British Library, comes from Tudor times. It could be substituted with any available facsimile, preferably linked to accessible CD recordings. Photocopies of manuscripts can be applied for directly or through libraries and plenty of books on music carry illustrations of original manuscripts. This one appears in Searle (1987).

This *In nomine* was probably written not long after the death of Henry VIII. Robert Parsons (c1530–1570) was a Gentleman of the Chapel Royal in London, from 1563 on and wrote music of all kinds – church music and other vocal music, instrumental music and dances.

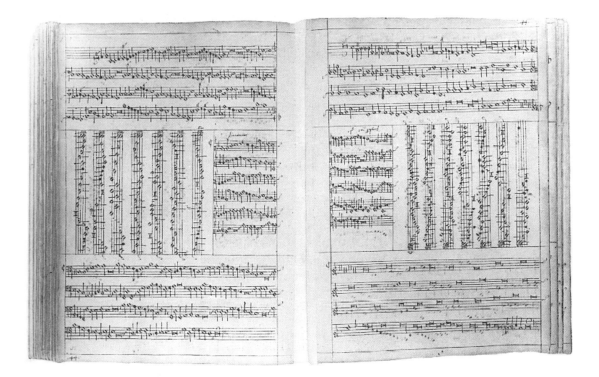

ADD MS 31390 ff24v,25. Reproduced by permission of The British Library.

activity ~ Look at the manuscript 'opening' above. What does it suggest to you about this piece and how it sounded? Give reasons for your ideas.

The music is written here as a table book, for players to stand or sit round when performing the music. It is not hard to imagine this scene in a Tudor household. There are parts for seven players, who play all at once. A close look shows one part in particular with differently drawn notes – the bottom left hand part has longer notes (no sticks). This is the part from which pieces of this kind derived their name, since it is a tune borrowed from a mass by John Taverner (c1495-1545). In its original setting the tune carried the words 'In nomine' and opened with the notes: D F D D D C F G and so on.

There were many other 'In nomine' pieces of this time (see CD: Fretwork); Brit. Mus. MS Add. 31390 includes forty two. The idea of borrowing a tune and building music round it in this way was a common one, which children can try for themselves. The other six instrumentalists play tunes that are all connected with the 'In nomine' itself. A useful discussion can be based on the question of what a composer gives seven different players to do if they all take part at once.

➤ Find out which instruments might have played this music, since none are specified. Use books (e.g. Ardley, 1989) or CD-ROMs and include looking at paintings of the time.

➤ Make up one or more small groups of players of similar instruments (e.g. recorders or strings) and try playing together. You might choose music of this time, another well known tune or round, or compose something yourself.

➤ Compare the sound of this group with a recording of a group playing Parson's music on period instruments. In what ways is it the same? different?

Henry VIII had a huge collection of instruments, both outdoor – such as sackbuts and trumpets, and indoor – such as viols and lutes. The most usual consort instruments for indoor domestic use were viols and recorders, each of which came as a family of different sizes. A chest of viols would contain 2 trebles, 2 tenors and 2 basses. A 'broken consort' consisted of a mixture of instrument families. As a longer term project, a small group of instrumentalists can investigate consort music of this period in the best way possible, by meeting regularly, sitting, as if round a table, and playing together.

individual progression

Children's progression through the 7–11 age-phase in relation to investigating music and the developing understanding and knowledge that this brings with it covers a major advance in capabilities and the potential for skill development. At the beginning of the age-phase, the level of each child's literacy and speaking and listening skills defines to a considerable extent the degree to which they can pursue musical investigations for themselves. Concepts of time and place may be quite shaky at the outset, but develop fast during this early phase, opening the way for much greater understanding of difference in relation to time, place and culture.

Individual children can draw on their own cultural experience, which will be musically diverse, and differentiation which maximises scope for this enables children to investigate music which is 'near home' in whatever sense and then share this with the class to strengthen independent work.

The greater ability to reflect on and understand social contexts which are beyond the child's own experience enhances the depth of investigative work towards the later part of the age-range. Independence in the use of sources and the ability to be more critical about their validity varies between individuals as do language skills, which by this time can be secure enough to use a wide range of reference material. There is much scope in allowing different members of a class to work to their strengths and pool findings; each child should feel able to contribute and be developing confidence in their own abilities to make sense of music.

assessment points

early stages

The child:
- can investigate music by listening, asking questions, and discussing how it is made;
- can use a range of sources to find out about music in relation to its context in time and place and the people who made it and can talk and write about their findings.

later stages

The child:
- can investigate music by listening, formulating questions, describing and analysing;
- can use a range of sources, including those demanding greater language skills, to investigate music of different times, places and cultures, and can reflect on and discuss findings through talking and writing.

primary music: later years

continuity and
progression

How can teachers make sure that the musical experience of each child moving through the school has both continuity and progression? At the same time, how can schools allow for children to follow individual pathways and to change and develop musically with confidence? Both are key issues if music learning is to be characterised by quality and high expectations for every pupil. They apply to any age-phase of school-based music education and the challenges they pose are real and difficult.

As we have seen, 7–11 is a wide age-range and a vital period for musical development. It is a stage during which many children formulate a view of themselves musically which remains with them for the rest of their life. And for many children it is framed by two major points of transfer. The first, from infants to juniors (in the English education system), coincides with a developmental watershed musically, as in other areas. This transfer often involves a change of school and will in nearly all cases be seen as the start of a new phase. The second is the transfer on into the secondary sector, into much larger schools and usually into a quite different kind of organisation. In addition, each year brings a move into a new class, with a new teacher carrying overall responsibility for progress.

As the child makes each of these transitions, music will not be the highest priority on the assessment and information agenda, crowded as it is with concerns about attainment in core areas, particularly literacy and numeracy, about behaviour, special learning needs and a range of personal information. The subject leader needs to plan realistically with colleagues so that points of transfer nevertheless carry some positive recognition of pupils' musical abilities, experience and interests so that there is the chance to build on these, opening up the next set of opportunities in a way that offers scope and challenge. Nothing is more de-motivating for pupils than the situation where at each point of transfer the teacher decides it is easier to 'start again'. The school as a whole must plan how to avoid this and it will depend on people and not paperwork. Continuity and progression can only be secured by high quality communication and interaction between teachers and pupils. Written records or schemes of work cannot begin to substitute for this.

individual progression

Achieving all this may require a fairly radical reappraisal of how music learning is seen. Some primary schools have excellent reputations for music which rest on a wide range of high-profile activities; yet they have no systems in place for monitoring the music learning and progress of each child as they pass through the school. The quality of experience may be extremely variable from child to child. Sometimes music is seen much more in terms of 'what we do' than of what she or he learns, and is carried out entirely on a basis of whole class or whole school activities (e.g. hymn practice, assembly listening) with over-reliance on a scheme or general plan and no differentiation across the range of abilities. This again can leave pupils with very poor provision in terms of learning progression.

If the priority is to be that of securing quality in music learning for each child, then the school as a whole must take a wide view of children's developmental needs in music and also recognise fully the range of different skills and knowledge involved in composing, performing, listening to and appraising music. It is not possible to manage music learning well unless it is accepted that children will take different pathways through the school's provision. (Examples of the kind of pathways individual progression might take have been included at the end of several sections of this book.)

Some children have individual or group lessons on a particular instrument in school or at home and may play that instrument in a group, band or orchestra. Some participate in a school choir, where they receive additional teaching of singing, or take solo voice parts in small or larger scale performances or dramatic productions. For others, learning to sing or play takes place only through the main curriculum. As composers, children may concentrate on different styles or genres of music according to their imagination and experience; as listeners it will be helpful to match some of their work to their music-making activities, for example, listening to music for the instrument they are learning, or to their developing tastes and interests – just as choice of reading will differ from child to child. This range of opportunity is crucial to high standards but it can make for difficulties in tracking progress. OFSTED reviews have recognised the complexity which can be involved in curriculum organisation for music and note that 'this complexity can make it difficult for headteachers and music co-ordinators to monitor the standards of attainment and progress of all pupils, and the quality with which music is taught throughout the school' (Mills, 1997).

So two issues run parallel: the need to maintain an overall continuity of experience for each child and the need for the monitoring of individual progress. In most subjects it is taken for granted that it is the individual progress made by each child that is monitored and assessed and that work is differentiated accordingly. Music is no different. The implications are that, in planning the organisation and the content of the music curriculum across the school, teachers must be clear about the kinds of progression envisaged and how learning is to be monitored.

assessment and progression

Progression is only secured by an approach to teaching which incorporates observing children, assessing their learning and adapting future activity to match their needs as demonstrated day to day and week to week. (Examples of points to notice have been indicated in relation to a range of activities in earlier sections of this book.) Any wider planning of work for the class across a half-term or longer will need to incorporate opportunities for all three processes: observation, assessment, and differentiation. Planning for continuity can then be founded on a realistic knowledge of the range of experience and attainment within any larger group of children. The idea of listening to individual children's work and assessing it against a framework of learning expectations in music is unfamiliar to many teachers, including specialists; it is, however, only an extension of the observational skills teachers draw on constantly in other areas. Critical listening and observation are the keys to high quality music teaching, far more so than abilities in instrumental technique or reading notation.

The assessment process must be rooted in all teaching, and children must be fully involved in it themselves. For each sequence of music work, the teacher will need to make clear to the children what learning is envisaged and where it belongs on the wider learning 'map'. When a shared and progressive approach is working well, many of the objectives will be derived from children's own perceptions of what is needed next and pupils can take a full part in identifying both general class objectives and personal learning targets. It is not always necessary to break work up into bite-size chunks although sometimes this is useful. In a single session the plan may just be to move a little further towards a rather longer term objective. Here pupils need to be clear in detail about the ways in which they will make progress towards the learning objective and what they need to contribute, think about, listen for, and practise. As work develops they can collaborate with the teacher in considering what they need to do in order to improve on a skill or extend their understanding. And they should be aware of the range of levels of accomplishment and be able to assess where they are individually or collectively on the way. This entails an understanding of what to listen or look for that will indicate how much has been achieved. At appropriate stages, time is kept for a review of learning against the original plan. This will include:

- learning planned for;
- additional learning;
- what the next step could be.

The key to any effective assessment is that teacher and pupils understand each other fully and that both engage in the process from the same understood basis. This grows out of day to day classroom interactions so that the processes and language of assessment are those in which learning takes place in the first instance.

If all this is in place, children will be able to take part fully in discussion of what has been learned and make their own self-assessments. They will be able to say what learning an activity involved, or what the challenge was in it, rather than just reporting what they 'did'. This enables learners to begin to develop their metacognitive understanding of the subject, knowing what they know with an additional layer of awareness of their own learning. This both increases their understanding and adds motivation and a sense of 'owning' their learning. Unfortunately, it runs strongly counter to some of the more traditional models of music learning, in which pupils 'do' many things, as instructed, without knowing why, or to where it is all leading, and with the teacher's ears alone used in judging progress.

On the basis of such an approach, making formative assessments becomes part of all teaching interactions. Making summative assessments, for example in order to report at the end of a year or age-phase, becomes much easier because the required information is all available. A teacher who has listened to, noticed and given feedback to individual children has little difficulty in making a summary report at a given point. A teacher who has planned work on a basis of clear and explicit objectives which have been shared with the children and readjusted as work progresses has a ready-made framework against which to assess and report achievement and difficulties. Assessment becomes problematic only to the degree that it is separated from the main activity of teaching.

It is not only assessment that falls more easily into place once time is allowed for the strategies outlined here. Genuine progression, together with a sense of achievement, is to a large extent the outcome of a good match between pupils' capabilities and needs and teaching and learning activity. A quality approach to assessment makes such a match possible and answers many of the questions about 'how to go on'. Lastly, once pupils have a clear understanding of their own learning, they have a basis for sustaining their own sense of continuity. For children, learning to stop, look back, and review progress over a longer stretch contributes greatly to their sense of achievement and growing independence. Music notebooks which are added to regularly and annual music profiles, presented in verbal formats, annotated drawings, or taped interviews help to give a tangible form to this.

developing continuity

Clearly teachers need school-wide agreement about the music learning 'map' against which to set their observations; becoming familiar with this may need to be a target in school curriculum development plans. Continuity can be helped enormously if the vocabulary used for talking about music is consistent throughout the school. Staff listening together to samples of children's work and discussing the evidence of learning which they give is a useful strategy. Knowing how to move children on rests on being able to take cues from the results of their work; once this is happening, progression begins to take shape. A project in which every teacher carries out a jointly planned unit of music work, adapting it for their own class age-group and comparing results together afterwards can be an excellent way of developing a sense of both developmental factors and how to teach for progression. It also contributes to the sense of a common vision for music across the school, which is fundamental to continuity.

Once a sense of individual pathways and expected progression is in place, planning for music year by year across the school becomes much simpler. Instead of trying to secure progression by sequencing activities in order of 'difficulty', a strategy which is doomed from the start, teachers are able to approach the development of skills and understanding by adapting levels of work appropriately, whatever the chosen content. Some way of tracking work covered, music played, sung and listened to with each class can be established, so that this basic information also accompanies each class as it moves through the school, avoiding overlap. This can be difficult where children are re-grouped in different ways. Sometimes two-year cycles of repertoire are needed to cover classes in which children stay longer. An individual child's pathway should not encounter repeated restarts with the same material unless there is a good reason for doing so.

points of transfer

A similar diagnostic approach is needed to ensure continuity at points of transfer, both between classes and across schools. Reporting on music may contribute here but receiving teachers can usefully plan early encounters with a new class in such a way as to allow children to show their capabilities and understanding. A jointly planned 'bridging' project, started at the end of one year and finishing at the beginning of the next is one way. Any of the following activities might be useful diagnostic starters to a new year, with the aim of giving observation and assessment opportunities.

activities

~ Plan a sequence of circle games and short activities which cover listening skills, singing, playing, and talking. *Use these to observe the range of skills among the class and also to begin to pinpoint individual children's abilities.*

~ Make a class tape of songs the children know, either that everyone knows or that a small group or soloist can sing by themselves; this can be lodged in the classroom for general listening or swapped with another class, or community group. *This incorporates a certain amount of debate about repertoire, an indication of different levels of skill and independence in singing and an opportunity to hear how children appraise their work when the tape is listened to.*

~ Make a tape 'radio' programme in which individual children are interviewed about their choice of music, telling the listeners something about it; or have a DJ spot from time to time when individual children introduce and play a piece of their choice. *This encourages children to talk about music in different ways; it helps to establish how much musical vocabulary children have as well as something of their preferences and knowledge.*

The effectiveness of diagnostic work of this kind rests on the quality of teaching interactions with children, on making sure that children are given opportunities to demonstrate their capabilities and not pre-judging these too hastily.

Continuity involves sustaining opportunities for children over time. It depends on presenting these in such a form that children can make their own connections and make sense of new work in relation to old. Children should be clear about their own past musical achievements, confident in their current sense of themselves musically, and articulate about where their particular musical strengths and creative concerns might take them next. They will experience continuity when they recognise new learning territory as a different place but on a familiar map, when they can look back and remember where they've been, and see how they got here. Teaching children in such a way that they can represent themselves accurately, through what they can do and what they can say, is the best way of all to ensure continuity. The child, after all, *is* the continuity; children, like everyone else, carry their learning with them.

early stages

The child:
- can control the pitch of their voice across a range appropriate for standard children's songs and knows some simple principles of voice technique;
- can join in simple voice games and improvised activities in which one voice sings independently to another;
- composes songs with some understanding of song forms;
- can distinguish a range of instrumental sound, and describe the sound and how it is made;
- can compose imaginative music for single instruments, and for two players, matching the music to the instrument's capabilities;
- understands a range of ways in which music can be composed for one, two or more instruments and can talk about texture in relation to other elements;
- can perform instrumental music alone and with a partner, keeping together and listening to each other;
- can dance with music keeping to the beat using simple travelling steps at a moderate speed;
- knows some different styles of dancing and dance music and can talk about dance music using simple terms;
- shows, through composing, listening and performing, a developing sense of the power of bringing music together with words and drama;
- can investigate music by listening, asking questions, and discussing how it is made;
- can use a range of sources to find out about music in relation to its context in time and place and the people who made it and can talk and write about their findings.

later stages

The child:
- can control the voice appropriately in singing a repertoire of songs across a range of styles;
- can maintain a simple voice part with a partner who is singing a different melodic part;
- composes and performs songs showing creativity and a sensitivity to combinations of words and music;

- can listen to music for one, two or more parts, beginning to be able to follow the lines separately and together, and describe the timbres and textures used;
- can compose imaginative music for a range of single instruments, including for another player to perform, showing knowledge of the instruments' potential and capabilities; can compose music for two or more players, making decisions based on some understanding of texture in part music;
- can appraise instrumental music by other composers, making comparisons of the different ways music for one, two or more parts can be structured;
- can perform instrumental music alone and in a group, showing listening and ensemble skills;
- can dance in time with music using a variety of movements and across a wide range of speeds;
- knows a number of different dances from other times and places; can talk about dance music using musical terms to describe the musical elements of duration, metre, tempo and form;
- has developed a range of understanding and skills in using music in relation to words and drama;
- can investigate music by listening, formulating questions, describing and analysing;
- can use a range of sources, including those demanding greater language skills, to investigate music of different times, places and cultures, and can reflect on and discuss findings through talking and writing.

books and resources

Adams, P. (1997) *Sounds Musical*. Oxford: OUP.

Ardley, N. (1989) *Eyewitness Guides: Music*. London: Dorling Kindersley.

Bagenal, A. and M. (1993) *Music from the Past*. Oxford: OUP.

Bean, J. and Oldfield, A. (1991) *Pied Piper: Musical Activities to develop basic skills*. Cambridge: CUP.

Cotton, M. (1996) *Agogo Bells to Xylophone: a friendly guide to classroom percussion instruments*. London: A and C Black.

Davies, L. (1994) *Take Note*. BBC Publications.

Durrant, C. and Welch, G. (1995) *Making Sense of Music*. London: Cassell.

East, H. (1989) *The Singing Sack*. London A and C Black.

East, H. (1990) *Look Lively, Rest Easy*. London: A and C Black.

Gilbert, J. (1997) *European Festivals*. Oxford: OUP.

Glover, J. and Ward, S. eds (1999) *Teaching Music in the Primary School*. London: Cassell.

Hennessy, S. (1995) *Music 7–11*. London and New York: Routledge.

Hennessy, S (1998) *Co-ordinating Music across the Primary School*. London: Falmer Press.

Kerr, S. (1994) *The Song Sampler*. Folkworks.

Mills, J. (1995) *Music in the Primary School* (2nd edition). Cambridge: CUP.

Nothants. C.C. (1996) *A Guide for Teachers Using Technology in Music*. Northants: NIAS Products and Sales.

OFSTED (1998) *The Arts Inspected*. Oxford: Heinemann

Pugh, A. (1991) *Women in Music*. Cambridge: CUP.

Richards, C. (1995) *Listen to This! Key Stage 2*. Gloucs.: Saydisc Records.

Roberts, T. ed. (1995) *Encouraging Expression: The Arts in the Primary Curriculum*. Special Needs in Ordinary Schools. London: Cassell.

Sanderson, A. ed. (1995) *Banana Splits: ways into part singing*. London: Cassell.

Shreeves, R. (1991) *Children Dancing*. London: Ward Lock Educational.

Young, S. and Glover, J. (1998) *Music in the Early Years*. London: Falmer.

Primary Music Today Magazine: Peacock Press, Scout Bottom Farm, Mytholmroyd, Hebden Bridge, HX7 5JS.

references

music 7-11
Young, S. and Glover, J. (1998) *Music in the Early Years*. London: Falmer Press.

musical awareness
Elliott, D.J. (1995) *Music Matters: A New Philosophy of Music Education*. Oxford: Oxford University Press.
Sartre J. P. (1940/1972) *The Psychology of the Imagination*. London: Methuen.
Schafer R. M. (1975) *The Rhinoceros in the Classroom*. Canada: Universal Edition.
Sloboda, J. (1985) *The Musical Mind*. Oxford: Clarendon.
Willems, E. (1971) *Les Bases Psychologiques de L'Education Musicale*. Bienne, Switzerland: Editions Pro Musica.
Young, S. and Glover, J. (1998) *Music in the Early Years*. London: Falmer Press.

music for voices
books
Brewer, H. (1995) 'Sexism and Stereotype in the Text of Children's Songbooks', *Primary Music Today: Issue 2* Hebden Bridge: Peacock Press.
Broughton, S. et al. (1994) *World Music: The Rough Guide*. London: The Rough Guides.
Cooksey, J. and Welch, G.F. (1997) 'Adolescence, singing development and national curricula design', *British Journal of Music Education*. 14(3) Cambridge: Cambridge University Press.
Kerr, S. (1997) 'Composing songs at Key Stage 2', *Primary Music Today: Issue 9*. Hebden Bridge: Peacock Press.
Kirwan, B. (1997) 'New songs for old', *Primary Music Today: Issue 8*. Hebden Press: Peacock Press.
Randall, L (1996) *Annie Lennox* Interview disc and book. Carlton SAM 7013
Titon, J.T. (1992) (ed.) *Worlds of Music: An Introduction to the Music of the World's Peoples*. New York: Schirmer.
[book: ISBN 0-02-872602-2 compact disc package: ISBN 0-02-872605-7]
Welch, G.F. (1997) 'The developing voice', L. Thurman and G.F. Welch (eds) *Bodymind and Voice*. Iowa: National Center for Voice and Speech.
Young, S. and Glover, J. (1998) *Music in the Early Years*. London: Falmer Press.

music
Britten, B. (1966) *Friday Afternoons*. London: Boosey and Hawkes.
Canon in Honour of Henry VIII. British Library, ROYAL MC 11 E.XI,ff2V,3.
Goetze, M. (1984) *Simply Sung: Folk Songs Arranged in Three Parts for Young Singers*. London: Schott.
Hillier, P. (1987) (ed.) *The Catch Book: 153 Catches Including the Complete Catches of Henry Purcell*. Oxford: Oxford University Press.
Kerr, S. (1994) *The Song Sampler: 26 Folk Songs from Around the World for Group Singing*. Newcastle: Folkworks.
[69, Westgate Road, Newcastle upon Tyne, NE1 1SG (includes free cassette)]
Landeck, B. (1961) *Echoes of Africa in Folk Songs of the Americas*. New York: David McKay Company, Inc.
LeFanu, N. (1984) *Rory's Rounds: Thirteen Rounds for Young Singers*. London: Novello.

compact discs
Achanak (tracks 1, 6, 12,13) East 2 West: Bhangra for the Masses. Music Club/Nachural Records MCCD 121
Adzido, Pan African Dance Ensemble, Siye Goli. EUCD 1223

Bulgarian State Television Female Vocal Choir, Ritual: Le mystere des Voix
Bulgares. Elektra Nonesuch, Explorer Series 7559-79349
Celia Cruz , Melao De Cana MCCD 220
Enya, Watermark. WEA Records Ltd 2292-43875-2
Marta Sebestyen, *The Best of Marta Sebestyen.* Hannibal: LC 7433
Sheila Chandra, *ABoneCroneDrone*. RealWorld 0 1704-62356-2
Sweet Honey in the Rock, *I Got Shoes*: Music for Little People. P.O. Box 1460
Redway California 95560-1460 [available HMV]
Rough Guide to World Music on CD: World Music Network
Voices of the World: An anthology of vocal expression. CMX 374 1010.12

music for instruments
books
Ben Tovim, A. (1979) *Children and Music.* London: A and C Black.
Bruce, R. and Kemp, A. (1993) 'Sex-stereotyping in Children's Instrumental
Preferences', *British Journal of Music Education 10.3.* Cambridge: Cambridge
University Press.
Sachs, C. (1940) *The History of Musical Instruments.* New York: Norton.
O'Neill, S. (1997) *'Gender and Music'* in Hargreaves, D.J. and North, C. (eds)
The Social Psychology of Music. Oxford: Oxford University Press.
Young, S. and Glover, J. (1998) *Music in the Early Years.* London: Falmer Press.

compact discs
Bach, J. S. *3 sonatas and 3 partitas for violin* (Elizabeth Wallfisch, complete)
Hyperion CDD22009 and 6 *Suites for cello* (YoYo Ma, complete). Sony S2K37867
Berio, Luciano *Sequenza I – flute* (Nicolet) WER6021-2. *Sequenza V – trombone*
(Lindberg) BIS-CD388. *Sequenza VII – oboe* (Holliger). PHIL 426 662-2PSL
Britten, Benjamin *Gemini Variations* (Jeney and Jeney). LOND CD 436 393-2LM
Debussy, Claude *Syrinx* (Phillippa Davies), Virgin VC7 59604-2
Fitkin, Graham *Stub* (Delta Saxophone Quartet), *Hook* (Ensemble Bash). Decca
argo 440 216-2
Reich, Steve *Clapping Music* (The Sixteen). COLL 1287-2
Xenakis, Iannis *Pleiades* (Les Percussions De Strasbourg). harmonia mundi. HMC
905185.
Shakuhachi music on *Japan: Traditional vocal and instrumental music*. Electra
Nonesuch Explorer series 972072-2
Music of the Andes, Caliche. Saydisc CD-SDL 388
Abe, Keiko *Michi* for marimba on Evelyn Glennie – *Wind in the Bamboo Grove*
Catalyst. 09026 681932
Hasidic melody 4 on *Raisins and Almonds* (Lucie Speaking and Burning Bush).
Jewish Songs from the Ashkenazi and Sephardic Traditions. Say disc CD SDL 395

maximising opportunities
Storr, A. (1992) *Music and the Mind.* London: Harper Collins.
Sugrue, C. (1997) *Complexities of Teaching: Child-centred perspectives.* London:
Falmer Press.

music, dance and drama
books and articles
Cohen, S.J. (1992) (Ed.) *Dance as a Theatre Art: Source readings in dance history
from 1581 to the present. Second edition.* Princeton, NJ: Princeton Book Company.
Katsarova, R. (1951) *Dances of Bulgaria.* London: Max Parrish and Company.
Kwami, R.M. (1986) 'A West African Folktale in the Classroom', *British Journal of
Music Education* 3 (1). Cambridge University Press: Cambridge.
Loane, B. (1984) 'On 'Listening' in music education', *British Journal of Music*

Education, **1** (1).
Opie, I. and Opie, P. (1985) *The Singing Game*. Oxford: Oxford University Press.
Rolfe, L. and Harlow, M. (1997) *Let's Look at Dance!* London: Fulton.
Sendak, M. (1963) *Where the Wild Things Are*. London: Bodley Head.
Tomlison, K. (1972) *The Art of Dancing*. New York: Dance Horizon.
Upton, E. and Paine, L. (1996) *Up the sides and down the middle: traditional English folk dance*. Exmouth: Southgate Publishers.
Woods, P. and Jeffrey, B. (1996) *Teachable Moments: the art of teaching in primary schools*. Buckingham: Open University Press.

Compact discs
Adams, John *Nixon in China*. Elektra Nonesuch 9 79177-2
Altan *The Best of Altan*. Green Linnet Records GLCD 1177
Britten, Benjamin *A Midsummer's Night's Dream*, Virgin Classics DDD 0 777 7 59305 2 8, *Noyes Fludde*. Virgin Classics UV 7243 5 61122 2 3, *Peter Grimes*. Decca 414577-2
Ensemble Eduard Melkus *Dance Music Through the Ages*. Archiv Production: 439 964-2
Fiddle Sticks: Irish Traditional Music from Donegal. Nimbus NI5320
Folk music of Bulgaria: collected and edited by A.L. Lloyd. Topic world series: TSCD 905
Folk music of Greece: collected and edited by W. Dietrich. Topic world series: TSCD 907
Hildegard *Ordo Virtutum* (Sequentia). deutsche harmonia mundi Edito Classica GD77051
Magic Bali *Le Ramayana*. Gamelan and Ketjak Playasound PS65003
Monk, Meredith *The Tale*. KOCH International Classics 3-7104-2 HI
Monteverdi *Orfeo*. harmonia mundi HMC90 1553/4
Mozart *The Magic Flute*. Phillips 426 276-2
Reich, Steve *Different Trains* (Kronos). Elektra Nonesuch 979 176-2
Purcell *Dido and Aeneas*. harmonia mundi HMX290 1528/33
Sondheim, Stephen *Sunday in the Park with George*. RCA CD. RD85042
Village Music of Yugoslavia: songs and dances from Bosnia-Herzegovina, Croatia and Macedonia. Nonesuch Explorer series. H-72042
Weir, Judith *King Harald* and *The Consolations of Scholarship*. Novello NVLCD 109

For further research

Education Dept. English Folk Dance and Song Society
Cecil Sharp House
2, Regent's Park Road
LONDON NW1 7AY (0171 485 2206)

music tools
Goehr, L. (1992) *The Imaginary Museum of Musical Works*. Oxford: Oxford University Press.
Robinson, G. (1995) *Sketchbooks: Explore and Store*. London: Hodder and Stoughton.

investigating music
books
Ardley, N. (1989) *Music* (Eyewitness Guides). London: Dorling Kindersley.
Blacking, J. (1987) *A commonsense view of all music*. Cambridge: Cambridge University Press.
Ekdahl Davidson, A. ed. (1992) *The Ordo Virtutum of Hildegard of Bingen*.

Michigan University: Medieval Institute Publications.

Fox, M, (1985) *Illuminations of Hildegard of Bingen*. Michegan University: Bear & Co.

Pugh, A. (1991) *Women in Music*. Cambridge: Cambridge University Press.

Sadie, J. and Samuel, R. (1994) *The New Grove Dictionary of Women Composers*. London: Macmillan.

Young, S. and Glover, J. (1998) *Music in the Early Years*. London: Falmer Press.

music

Davison, A. and Apel, W. (1946) *Historical Anthology of Music Vol 1*. London: Oxford University Press.

Robert Parsons *In nomine*. British Library: ADD MS 31390 ff24v,25.

For an easily obtainable performing score of *The Play of Daniel* see Greenberg, N. (ed.) (1964) Oxford: Oxford University Press.

compact discs

Bill Evans *Conversation with Myself*. Verve 521 409-2

Hildegard of Bingen – Sequentia – *Canticles of Ecstasy*. deutsche harmonia mundi 05472 77320-4; *Voice of the Blood* 05472 77346-2

In Nomine English Music for viols – Fretwork. Amon-Ra CDSAR29 contains *In Nomines* by Baldwin, Bull, Byrd, Ferrabosco, John Johnson, Parsons (in 5 parts), Tallis, Taverner, and Tye.

Musical Instruments CD-ROM. Microsoft.

The Play of Daniel (Ludus Danielis). CHR77144

continuity and progression

Mills, J. (1997) 'OFSTED Music Inspection Findings 1995-6' in *Primary Music Today. Issue 8*. Hebden Bridge: Peacock Press.

index